SWEEP PICKING
SPEED STRATEGIES FOR
7-STRING GUITAR

Discover Seven-String Guitar Arpeggios, Techniques and Licks

CHRIS BROOKS

FUNDAMENTAL CHANGES

Sweep Picking Speed Strategies For 7-String Guitar

Discover Seven-String Guitar Arpeggios, Techniques and Licks

ISBN: 978-1-78933-079-3

Published by **www.fundamental-changes.com**

Copyright © 2019 Christopher A. Brooks

Edited by Tim Pettingale & Joseph Alexander

www.fundamental-changes.com

Twitter: @guitar_joseph

Over 10,000 fans on Facebook: **FundamentalChangesInGuitar**

Instagram: **FundamentalChanges**

For over 350 Free Guitar Lessons with Videos Check Out

www.fundamental-changes.com

Contents

Introduction

While there are a few books that do a decent job of teaching sweep picking on guitar, in my 25 years of teaching I've come across hundreds of students who understand the concept but still fail to get the sound they want.

While the process of brushing the pick through *arpeggios* or *broken chords* with single downstrokes or upstrokes seems straightforward enough, it's only one piece of the puzzle. It's time for a method that develops an all-encompassing approach to creating efficient arpeggio lines and incorporates all the necessary bio-mechanics and nuance of pick control.

As a teacher, I'm constantly asked the following:

How do I make it sound good?

How do I control the noise?

Why does one direction feel easier than the other?

What should I do when there's more than one note on a string?

How do I change direction?

How do I get beyond triads?

Why don't I sound as good as Jason Becker, Vinnie Moore or John Petrucci?

Questions like these warrant a more comprehensive approach than a book of drills, so rather than cutting straight to the licks, this book will get you thinking about the quantum of factors affecting your results, and how to make them all work for you. From rudiments to extensive fretboard coverage, this book outlines a whole system you can use to become an incredible sweep picker.

Beyond laying out the essential principles of sweeping technique and the tools for developing it, this method presents you with options, explain the outcomes of the choices you make along the way, and encourages you to systemise your strengths into a personalised approach.

Most of the chapters conclude with practice or goals to accomplish before moving ahead. Practice methods will vary significantly from player to player, but these summaries will tell you what to expect in each of the stages of learning, and how to approach your workout sessions for the best results.

As this is a seven-string adaptation of my existing sweep picking book, you'll find shapes and strategies equally suited to the first six strings, but with exclusive additional content to explore the benefits and challenges of the extended range for both standard and drop-tuned seven-string guitar.

Chapters One to Ten notate shapes and examples in standard seven-string tuning (B-E-A-D-G-B-E) while Chapter Eleven is all about adaptation strategies for Drop A tuning, with shapes to match.

Thanks for once again entrusting me to be your guide. Enjoy the process of building your seven-string technique and vocabulary for arpeggios.

Chris Brooks

Get the Audio

The audio files for this book are available to download for free from **www.fundamental-changes.com.** The link is in the top right-hand corner. Simply select this book title from the drop-down menu and follow the instructions to get the audio.

We recommend that you download the files directly to your computer, not to your tablet, and extract them there before adding them to your media library. You can then put them on your tablet, iPod or burn them to CD. On the download page, there is a help PDF, and we also provide technical support via the contact form.

For over 350 Free Guitar Lessons with Videos Check out:

www.fundamental-changes.com

Twitter: **@guitar_joseph**

Over 10,000 fans on Facebook: **FundamentalChangesInGuitar**

Instagram: **FundamentalChanges**

Chapter One: Rudiments of Flow

Regardless of your musical style or experience, all players can incorporate efficiency, flow, tone and timing into sweep picking. As readers of my first book, *Neoclassical Speed Strategies for Guitar* will note, there are commonalities between the biomechanics of that system and the ones required for good sweep picking.

I break the development of sweep picking into six rudiments:

1. Pick edge offset

2. Rest strokes

3. Directional pick slants

4. Turning mechanics

5. Fretting hand timing

6. String control

You may already have some of these in place, but let's progress through each in the suggested order.

Pick Edge Offset

Creating a flowing sweep starts from the moment the pick approaches the string. Angling the pick horizontally (or Pick edge offsetting) allows either the outer or inner edge of the pick to lead the contact with the string, avoiding friction that might be created by using its full flat face. (*on-axis*).

Pick edge offsets are *off*-axis positions created by your wrist placement and pick grip. There is no right or wrong way to twist the pick off axis to the string, but some approaches are more common than others.

If you use the pad of the thumb and the side of the index finger to hold the pick, *outer edge offset* (Figure 1a) might feel the most natural to you. The edge of the pick that faces away from the hand is what contacts the strings first on downstrokes.

Notable sweep pickers with this grip and offset include Vinnie Moore, Paul Gilbert, Michael Romeo, Yngwie Malmsteen, Jason Becker and Frank Gambale. Among them, you might see varying degrees of bending in the joints of the thumb and index finger, so do your homework on your favourite pickers. Examine and emulate!

If your pick is held with more pad of the index finger than the previous description, *inner edge offset* (Figure 1b) is the most likely to occur, with the inside edge of the pick contacting first a downstroke. You might also see some concave bending of the thumb.

Right-handed players can also consider outer and inner edge-leading to be *clockwise* and *anti-clockwise* offsets respectively, with the opposite being true for left-handed players.

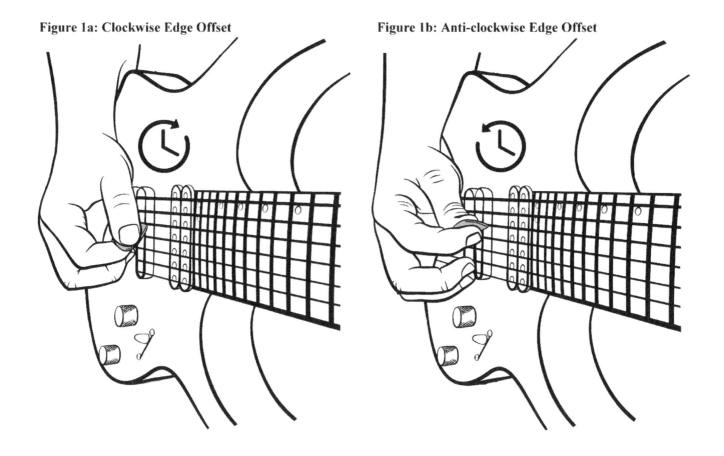

Figure 1a: Clockwise Edge Offset

Figure 1b: Anti-clockwise Edge Offset

Some players have an unusual *mix and match* of approaches (Marty Friedman and John Norum, for example), so don't feel pressured to fit into one category or the other. Examine the amount of friction your pick creates against the string and incorporate a degree of pick edge offset to minimise it.

Rest Strokes

Sweep picking is the technique of playing multiple notes with the same pick stroke but incorporating the *rest stroke* is the difference between a real sweep and a series of successive free strokes.

The rest stroke or *Apoyando* was popularised as a fingerstyle approach in the nineteenth-century and used for scale and melody work. Using Apoyando, the guitarist plucks upward with the fingers or downward with the thumb so that each stroke simultaneously lands and rests on the adjacent string.

Figure 1c: the thumb plucks the low E string and pushes into the A string; the index finger plucks the B string and pulls into the G string.

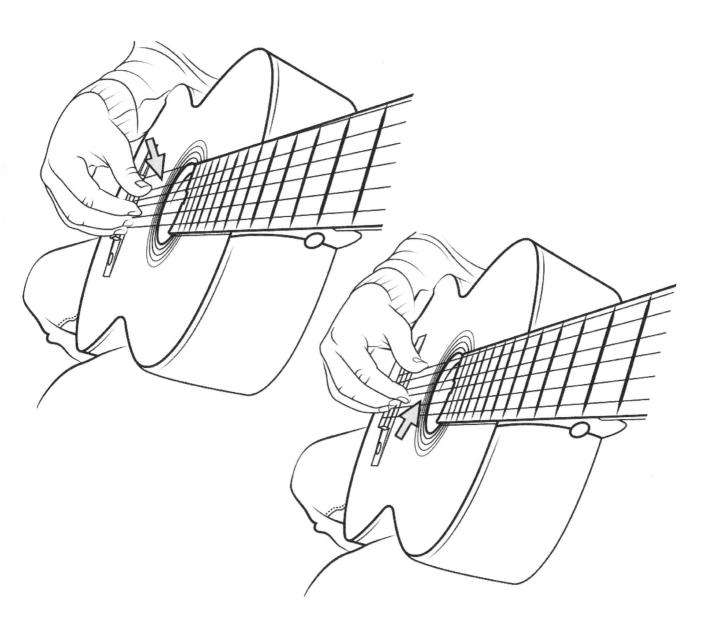

For us pickers, downstrokes and upstrokes in sweeping work the same way as the thumb and fingers in Apoyando. The rest stroke is accomplished by following each pick stroke through to the next string. Each note will sound when leaving the string rather than when arriving at it.

During a downward sweep, upstrokes between notes are eliminated, as a single downstroke steps down to each new string. In an upward sweep the reverse occurs. Combined with directional pick slants and pick edge offsets, rest strokes enable economical, smooth and dynamically-consistent sweep picking.

Directional Pick Slants

Just like when strumming chords, sweep picking sees the pick working at two different angles for downstrokes and upstrokes as the pick snaps from one string to the next with rest strokes. These pathways are called pick slants, with the two angles nowadays referred to as *downward pick slant* and *upward pick slant* thanks to online educator Troy Grady.

Slanting is easily established using rotation of the forearm muscles, resulting in the picking hand turning outward or inward (Figure 1d). A downward slant is the result of outward rotation (supination) from the perpendicular or neutral position. An upward slant is the result of inward rotation (pronation) from the neutral position. Both slants push towards the guitar body on their way to the rest string.

Neoclassical Speed Strategies covers pick slant and picking orientation for scale playing in great detail, but for the purpose of sweep picking arpeggios, the concept of slanting can be condensed into two applications:

- Downward sweeping is done with a downward pick slant.

- Upward sweeping is done with an upward pick slant.

Slants work with rest strokes to create smooth contact with new strings and make directional changes possible without getting the pick trapped on the wrong side of a string.

Figure 1d: downward and upward pick slants

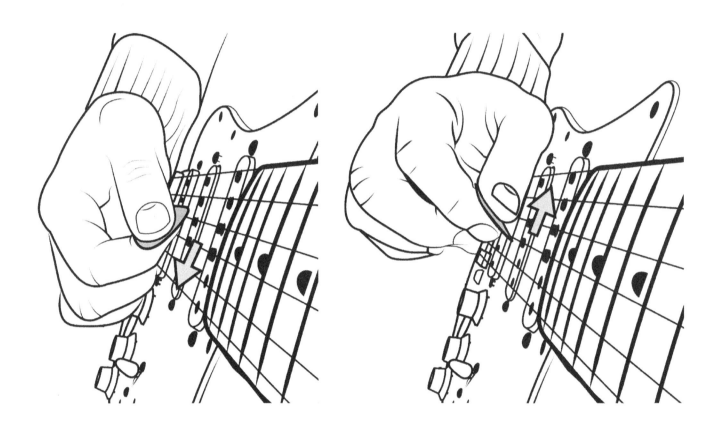

Understanding the Pick Slant Indicators in This Book

I've devised two markers to show pick slant directions for examples in this book:

\ **p.s.** for downward pick slant

/ **p.s.** for upward pick slant

When you can associate sweeping either direction with the applicable pick slant, you will no longer require the indicators. It's important to keep in mind that the locations of pick slant indicators are approximate. The re-orienting of the pick occurs smoothly just before the point it's notated. Avoid any robotic, jolting switches.

In Example 1a, you'll most likely feel yourself anticipating each new pick slant as you leave the previous note, so that the fully formed upward pick slant in bars one and three on beats 2 and 4 can be initiated coming out of the last 1/8th notes of beats 1 and 3. We'll discuss this in *Turning Mechanics* to ensure you avoid trapping the pick between strings when changing directions.

Example 1a:

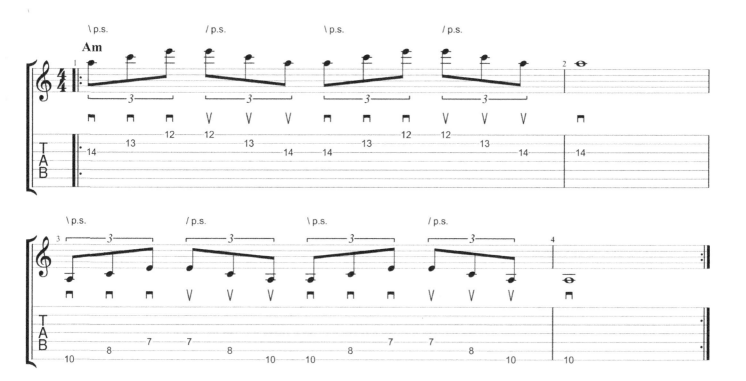

To develop your pick slant and rest stroke technique, start with Example 1b which uses muted strings on the fretting hand to allow complete focus on the picking hand. Each pick stroke should land on a new string the moment it leaves the previous one (excluding the final string in either direction, of course). The 1/16th rests allow time to change the pick slant in anticipation of the next sweep.

Example 1b:

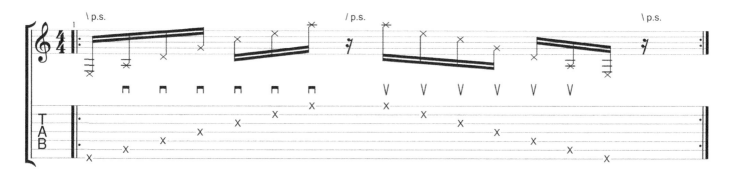

Turning Mechanics

Turning mechanics are the strategies that come into effect when an idea changes direction, repeats, skips strings, or any other factor that interrupts the directional flow of a sweep picking form.

The most common of these are the outside turn and the inside turn, which refer to picking around the strings in question (outside picking) or between them (inside picking). Despite the notion that sweep picking is about always choosing the shortest distance between two points, there are situations in which the effects of picking orientation produce some logical options worth considering.

Two terms I've created to help you relate turning mechanics to pick slants are *Upscaping* and *Downscaping*. Both refer to how we 'escape' the strings when changing direction.

Upscaping is escaping the strings with an upstroke in a downward pick slant i.e., pulling the pick away from the guitar. You'll be using that a lot in Chapter Two for repeating ascending sweeps.

Downscaping is the opposite: using a downstroke in an upward pick slant to escape the strings i.e., pushing the pick away from the guitar. You'll be using that in descending and bidirectional sweeps.

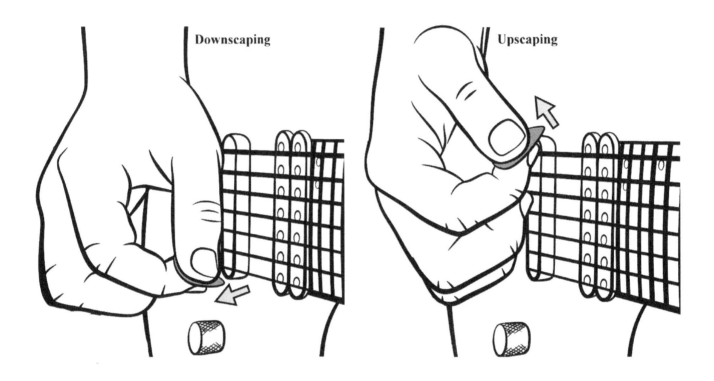

Fretting Hand Timing

Since arpeggios are used to create melody in this book, it's essential to develop clean, separated notes that neither overlap nor sound too choppy (staccato) when sweep picking. Fretting hand timing plays a role in this endeavour.

The two elements to be considered are synchronisation and duration. It's a common pitfall of the keen entry-level sweep picker to articulate the notes at the beginning and end of a broad arpeggio yet have a bunch of unarticulated mush in the middle! Hey, we've all been that kid in the music store on a Saturday!

Synchronisation must be a key goal, making sure that each pick stroke has a matching fretted note. Considering that the rest stroke technique sees the pick landing on each new string as soon as it leaves the previous string, the aim is not necessarily to have a fretted note ready on the rest string at that precise nanosecond, but by the moment the pick *leaves* the string. Remember that each note is articulated by the exit, not the entry to each step of the sweep.

If synchronisation is about *when* to arrive at a note, then duration is about *how long* to stay. Notes that overlap will sound chordal and perhaps unpleasant to the ear when play with distortion. In the opposite spectrum, notes changed too hastily may lose their fluid effect and seem disjointed. Unless otherwise intended as a musical choice, aim for arpeggios that sound smooth and pleasing to the ear.

String Control

The final rudiment of good sweep picking is string control which is achieved through a trio of *palm muting*, *palm rolling* and *fretting hand muting*. Mastering this three-pronged approach will help you create the desired articulation for the notes you play, and prevent unwelcome noise and sympathetic vibration from the other strings.

Existing in real performance, but difficult to represent in tablature alone, string control takes place in Example 1c across all strings, even with a small triad like this. On the low B, low E and A strings, palm muting is used to silence the strings placed geographically above the picking region.

Adjacent strings tend to elicit the most noise when sweep-picking arpeggios, so when fretting the C note on the 10th fret of the D string, use the pad of your second finger to contact and mute the G string below (Figure 1e). Don't apply pressure on that string in a barre form since you do not wish to sound a double-stop.

When you pick the 9th fret and 12th fret notes on the G string, the pads of the index and fourth fingers will mute the B string (and high E string if necessary). Depending on the size of your index finger, the very tip of the index finger may serve as a muting device for the D string at this point as well. Because of the cyclical nature of this lick, you may prefer to leave your index finger in place throughout the repeats.

Example 1c:

Figure 1e: the second finger frets the 4th string while muting the 3rd string.

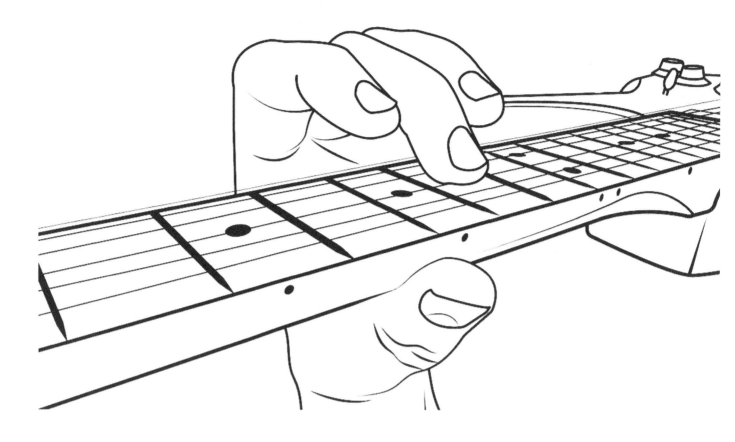

Applying the Picking Hand Palm Roll

Sweep picking across many strings requires great co-operation between picking hand and fretting hand muting. Expanding Example 1c by repeating the same fingering and picking form through three octaves, Example 1d requires the hands to work in opposites when muting.

In the lowest octave, apply no palm muting. Instead, use the underside of your fretting index finger to gently mute the higher strings (known as *across the board* muting). In the middle octave, a palm mute should fall into place on the low B and low E strings as the pick makes its way to the A string. In the highest octave, roll the palm muting to silence everything but the G and high B strings.

Practise this example with and without overdrive and listen out for any noise that needs to be addressed.

Example 1d:

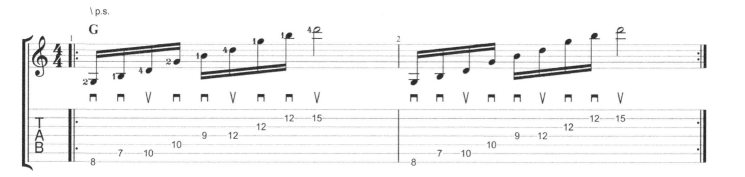

Palm rolling can also be used to add dynamic variation. In Example 1e, the G Major triad is articulated with alternating palm-muted and open sounds by rolling the mute on and away from the A and D strings. Listen to the audio to hear the contrast between open and muted picking.

Example 1e:

As with anything musical, the arbiter of success is in what you hear. As you build your sweep picking chops progressively through the chapters that follow, keep a critical ear on the sound of your arpeggios, and revise the fundamentals in this section whenever something does not sound clean and articulate.

Chapter Two: Ascending Strategy

In this chapter we will focus on the development and application of four components:

- Downward (ascending) sweep picking technique

- Downward rest stroke

- Downward pick slant

- Outside turning mechanic and upscaping

Using an A Minor triad (1, b3, 5), the ascending drills progress from two-string to seven-string sweeps in an expanding shape that will cover three octaves by the end of the chapter.

Shown below are two diagrams: the first shows the notes of the triad; the second indicates the fingers to be used throughout. Before sweeping, place the suggested fretting hand fingers on each of the notes, one at a time. Do so four to six times before you engage the picking hand in the first example.

A Minor

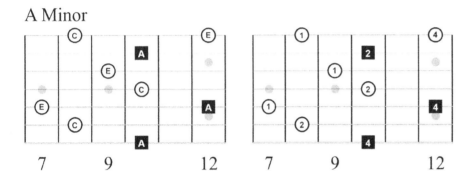

Example 2a starts with a downward sweep from the high B string to the high E string using a downward pick slant and a rest stroke. After pushing through the C note on the E string, a high E note on the same string is played with an upstroke. Palm muting must be used on strings three to seven.

By maintaining one pick slant throughout, the upstroke will pull the pick away from the guitar, upscaping back to the second string without any need to hop around it.

Example 2a:

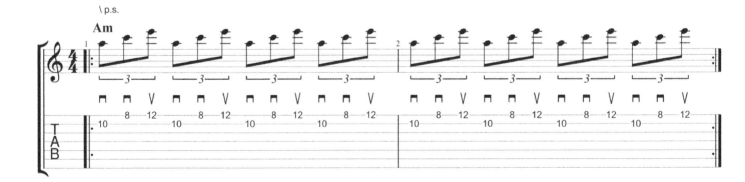

If the pick slant is ignored, the upstroke from the third note will trap the pick between the strings, creating the need for a secondary movement to bring the pick back to the starting point. The purpose of the pick slant is to avoid this problem.

An economy picker who encounters a triad like the above may bypass the outside turn mechanic from the high E string back to the B string, instead using an upward inside turn mechanic to use an up pick on the repeats.

This change creates a different picking form after the first downward sweep and is shown in Example 2b. This example is included to give you a broader sense of the options of sweep picking. This is covered in detail when we look at the descending approach in Chapter Four.

Example 2b (examine but don't practise just yet):

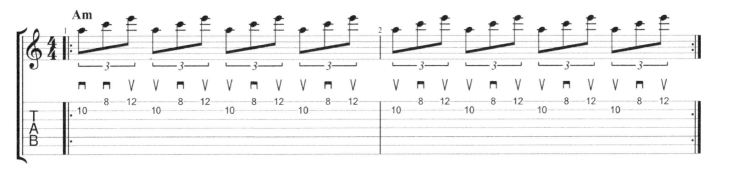

The looping nature of Example 2a means that the phrase can be melodically displaced without affecting picking mechanics, as demonstrated in Examples 2c and 2d. Displacement means that the same group of notes can be moved to different parts of the beat without affecting the optimal picking form.

Example 2c starts from the second note of the A Minor triad, and Example 2d begins on the third note.

For tidy notation, you'll often see examples like this written in 12/8 time rather than 4/4 with a constant stream of triplets. If you count aloud when you play, you can still vocalise the rhythm with *one-and-ah, two-and-ah* etc., as you would in 4/4.

Example 2c:

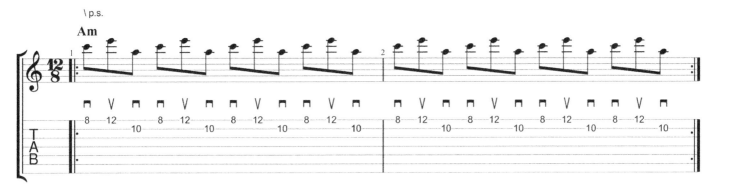

Beginning the next example with an upstroke might seem unusual at first, particularly if you've only ever alternate-picked things. However, with some practise, the benefits of mechanical consistency will pay off, negating the need for separate picking forms for each variation of the lick.

Example 2d:

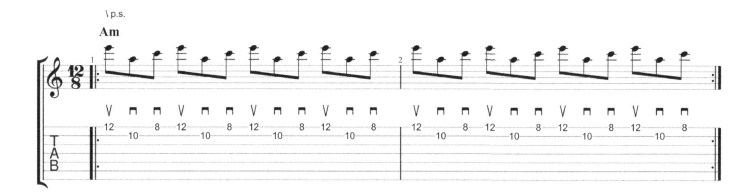

Expanding the arpeggio and sweep mechanic is merely a matter of adding an extra string. Example 2e sees the addition of an E note to the 9th fret of the G string.

Example 2e:

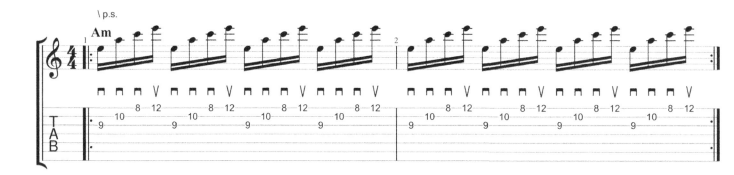

Displacing the previous example to start on the highest note of the triad with its associated upstroke, you may once again feel a little disorientation until you get the hang of it. Begin Example 2f very slowly, avoiding any timing discrepancies that might arise from having an extra downstroke note as the shape grows.

Example 2f:

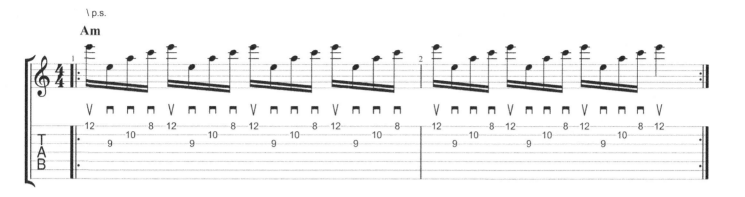

Extending the shape into the sweep pattern in Example 2g isn't very common due to the extended string leaps that occur in repetition. Example 2h remedies this with a figure that provides more time to get from the high E string back to the D string.

Example 2g:

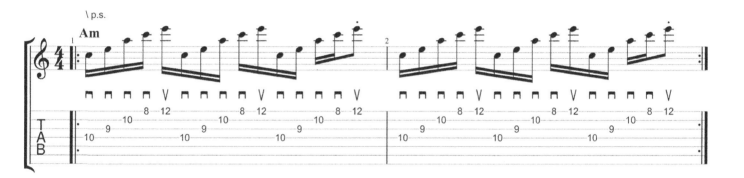

Example 2h:

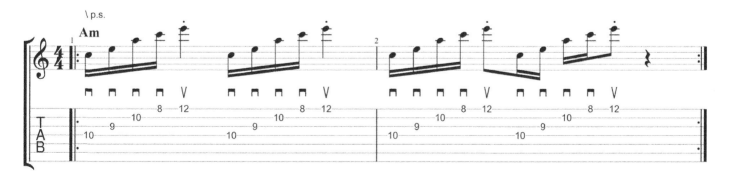

Example 2i consolidates the mechanics that you've acquired so far and the challenge is to maintain stable timing despite the distance of string jumps increasing as you work through each bar. Remember that any lick should only be played as fast as the most challenging part of it, so avoid rushing through beats 1 and 2 if it means slowing down in beats 3 and 4.

The two-string and three-string triads begin on beats 1 and 2 respectively but the four-string version starts on the second triplet of beat 3.

Example 2i:

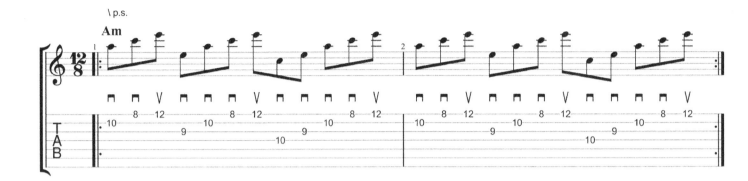

Since the five-string pattern uses the fourth finger for both the A root note on the A string and the E note on the high E string, it isn't feasible to launch into straight repeats with this shape. Instead, try integrating some other string groups, as outlined in Example 2j, which uses two and three string patterns.

With larger shapes, sweep picking can feel like trying to control a ball rolling down a hill. Avoid letting the timing get away from you as you mix sweeps in this drill.

Example 2j:

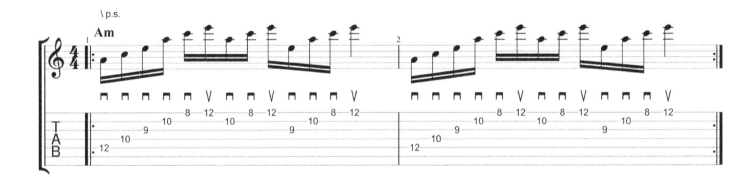

Musically, the next logical note to add to the A Minor triad is an E note below the A root. While the E note could be sourced from the 12th fret of the low E string, placing it on the 7th fret of the A string removes any fourth finger rolling that would have been necessary.

The shape now has two notes per string at either end, on the fifth and first strings, with three options for dealing with the A string, as spelt out in each bar of Example 2k.

1. Pick the two notes on the A string *down, up* and continue sweeping from the D string.

2. Pick the 7th fret of the A string with a downstroke, hammer on to the 12th fret and continue sweeping

3. Pick the two notes on the A string *up, down* with the downstroke sweeping through

Example 2k:

Which one is the best? For the sake of versatility, test all three and see what fits naturally into your style. I tend to alternate between the first two options. Option One has a consistent dynamic, being all picked, but Option Two is perhaps the least disruptive to pick stroke flow and involves the same number of strokes as the five-string ascent used in Example 2j. The rest stroke occurs between the first two downstrokes while the hammer-on takes place.

You can mix and match approaches according to the situation. For example, pick all the notes when staying within five strings, or use a hammer-on in the six-string form that you will see shortly in Example 2m.

The five-string *two at each end* shape works well in triplet rhythms like the one in Example 2l. This drill ascends through strings five to one, then doubles back for a two-string iteration in the second bar.

Example 2l:

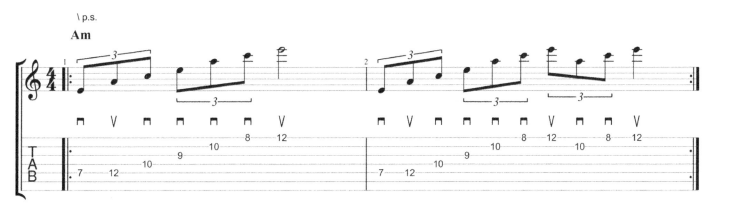

Another advantage of the layout used in Examples 2k and 2l is the finger-friendly extension now available on the low E string. By adding a C note on the 8th fret using the second finger, Example 2m extends from the low E string to the high E string with a single downstroke, using the hammer-on and an extended rest stroke on the A string to maximise the directional potential of the pick.

Example 2m:

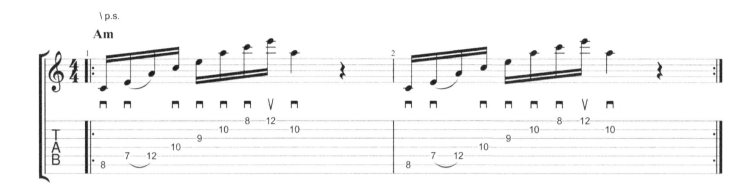

Building the A Minor triad in this position of the fretboard means that when it's time to expand to the seventh string, we now have a very stable sounding triad shape that represents each note three times across three octaves. It's a common shape for both sound and fingering ease.

In standard tuning, adding the A note to the 10th fret of the low B string gives us fingering familiarity since the shape on the seventh, six and fifth strings repeats on the fifth, fourth and third strings.

Example 2n:

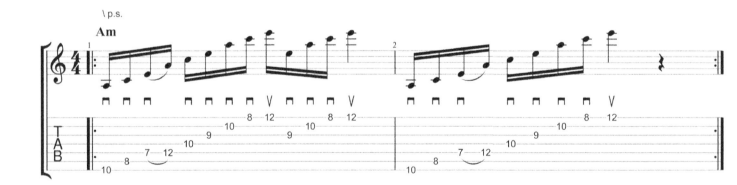

Practice and the three stages of motor learning

We have now built a method for growing two-string triads into seven-string sweeps while applying the technical fundamentals from Chapter One.

To solidify the examples taught so far, create a practice routine appropriate to your playing experience. If sweep picking is new to you, spend more developmental time on the smaller examples before adding strings.

Play each example in this chapter in free time a few times as an overview before adding the metronome. If you really need to focus on the picking hand, mute the strings with the fretting hand and try the picking pattern for each drill percussively at first, adding the pitched notes after a few runs through.

This is the *cognitive stage* of learning, where movements are slow and given much mental focus. In the cognitive stage, it's normal to feel like every aspect of a new skill is laborious. You are activating neural pathways that become strengthened through repetition. Ensure you're applying all the rudiments described in Chapter One.

On an average practice day, you might choose to work on three or four sweep picking drills in one session. Aim for at least twenty good repeats of an exercise before moving to the next. Do a few sets of twenty if you're keen. Forego the metronome just a little longer, since you should be focused on getting the motions fluid, efficient and consistent. When you can do this, you have reached the *associative stage*.

In the associative stage, tasks take less time to complete, require less conscious thought, and allow the multitasking of other elements of playing. You will notice that you have more freedom to consider what you are playing rather than simply how you are playing it. For example, you might find yourself focusing less on how to get the pick from one string to the next, and more about improving your tone and timing as you go. Everything you've learned on guitar so far has gone through this stage on its way from the cognitive process to autonomous freedom.

In the associative stage, you shouldn't be aiming for maximum speed (yet), but you will gain a useful insight into your progress by trying a burst of faster repeats, to see if your technique is ready to withstand some acceleration. If it's not, go back to *development speed,* but keep working those bursts from time to time.

As the first few drills get easier, shift your focus to new exercises, relegating accomplished material to warm-ups. For example, if you spent twenty minutes working on Examples 2a, 2c, 2d and 2e on Monday and Tuesday, spend five minutes revising them on Wednesday before having a focused session based on Examples 2f to 2i.

When you can play through each of the examples comfortably, take out the metronome and determine your *edge of ability* tempo (EOA). Your EOA tempo is the speed at which you can hold the lick together, just before the point of disintegration. Next, drop the metronome back to half of your EOA tempo and progressively work back up to maximum. For example, if your top speed for a lick is 100bpm, drop the metronome back to 50bpm, then work upwards in 10bpm increments when you can accurately play about ten repeats. At the end of the session, play in free time to the edge of your ability and see if your EOA tempo has increased against the metronome.

When you can play something fast in an almost automatic fashion, this is the *autonomous stage*. Your movements will be accurate and consistent. People refer to this as *muscle memory*, but muscles don't have a consciousness. It just means that your motor skills have reached an independent level.

Don't be discouraged if you can only bite off a few drills at a time, or if it takes weeks rather than days to see some gains. Practice is like physical exercise: a consistent program is the one that is likely to bring results. Trust and enjoy the process!

It's normal to have different drills spread simultaneously across the cognitive, associative and autonomous categories as you improve old drills while learning new ones. In general, however, getting better at even a few sweeping licks can advance the progress of other exercises that are in each stage of learning.

To mix things up for your ears, apply the ideas from this chapter to the major triad form (1, 3, 5) and practise each, adhering to the same picking patterns as the A Minor examples. This will allow you to start outlining common chord progressions involving major and minor sounds. The extended major triad looks like this:

A Major

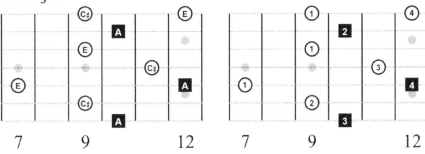

In the next section, you will be able to apply your new sweep chops to a range of etudes that are way more musical than static triads and will challenge your ability to change chords in time with the music.

Chapter Three: Ascending Etudes

In this section, the mechanical patterns of Chapter Two are applied to different chords and inversions to challenge the fretting hand and entertain the ears. Most of these have a somewhat *Neoclassical Rock* styling, but you can later apply the same picking forms to any chord progression or genre of your choice.

All shapes used are taken in part or whole from the Fretboard Coverage material in Chapter Eight. For now, just learn any new fingerings as they occur in each etude. There is nothing too complicated to worry about regarding fingering.

Be sure to maintain the fundamental principles when practising the drills from a slow pace to a brisk EOA tempo. In each example, apply your own preferences for muting and picking dynamics, and feel free to emulate my approaches from the audio. All the examples in this chapter use a downward pick slant.

To begin, Example 3a uses the two-string mechanic. The etude contains triads that start on either the root or 5th of the chord – the latter involving some index finger rolling across string pairs. Be careful not to play position rolls in a barre chord fashion with the notes audibly overlapping.

Bars one to four use the two-string mechanic on the D and G strings, changing octaves and strings to the high B and high E strings in bars five to eight.

Example 3a:

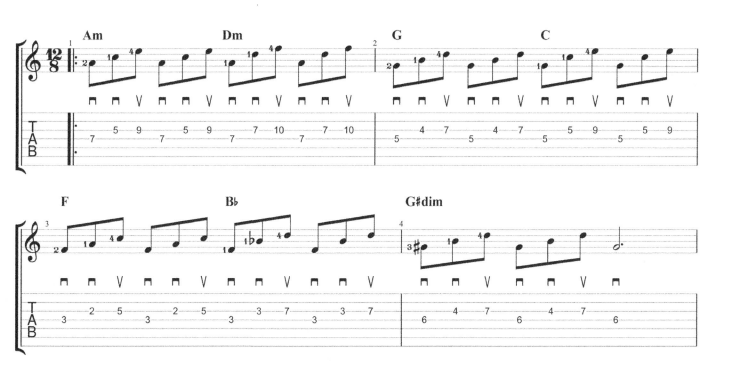

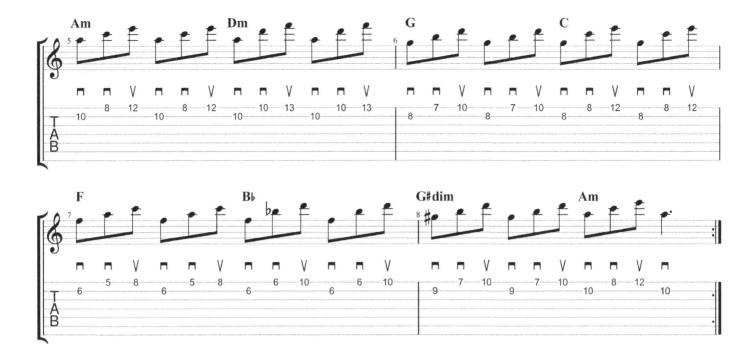

Advancing to three strings in Example 3b, a new shape is introduced at beat 3 of the first bar. This is an inversion of the previous A Minor triad. The second bar introduces a diminished triad shape with b3 and b5 degrees.

Example 3b:

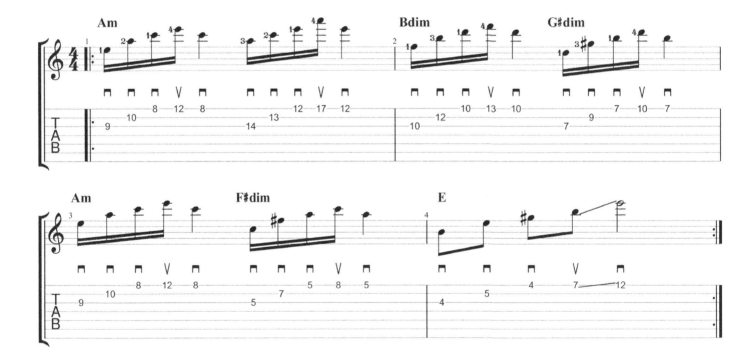

Example 3c brings together triads from the keys of C Major and C Minor. It's important to keep the *up, down, up* pick strokes in the second note grouping of each bar at the same speed as the downward sweeping that occurs within the beats on either side.

Example 3c:

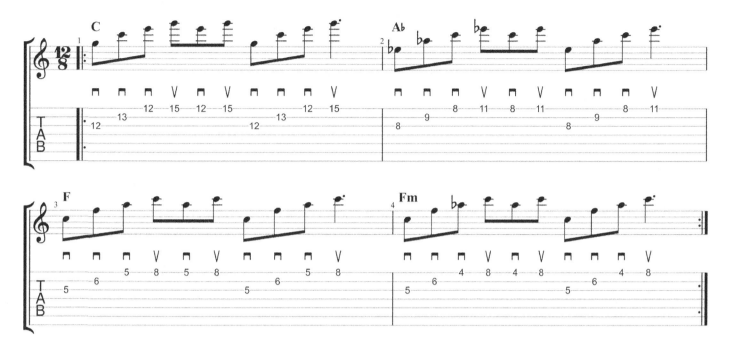

Example 3d begins and ends each bar on the D string (except for the last note in bar four), with two-string and three-string sweeps interwoven.

Example 3d:

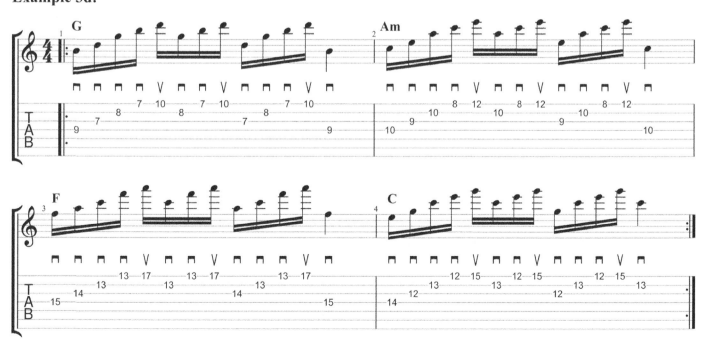

On five strings, Example 3e will put you through your paces with stretches and position jumps. Be sure that the timing of the hammer-ons does not waver.

Example 3e:

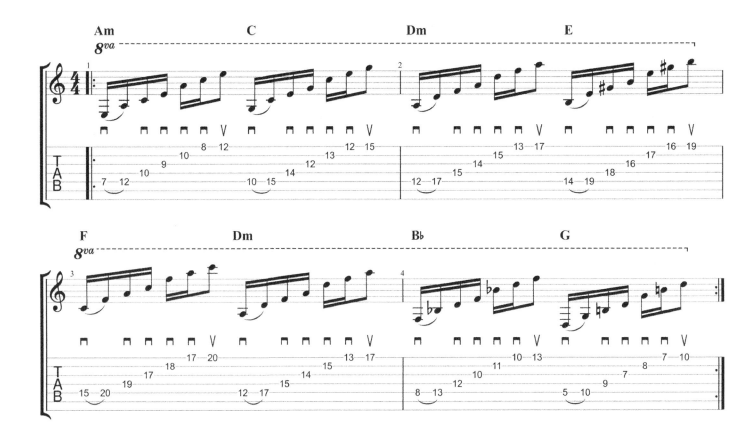

Example 3f applies six of the seven strings from the major triad shape at the end of Chapter Two through the chords C Major, Eb Major, F Major and F Minor. The first three notes of each bar are executed with *down, down, up* pick strokes with an outside string change back to the low E string. When the same three notes repeat on the way up to the high E string, two downstrokes and a hammer-on applied are employed.

Example 3f:

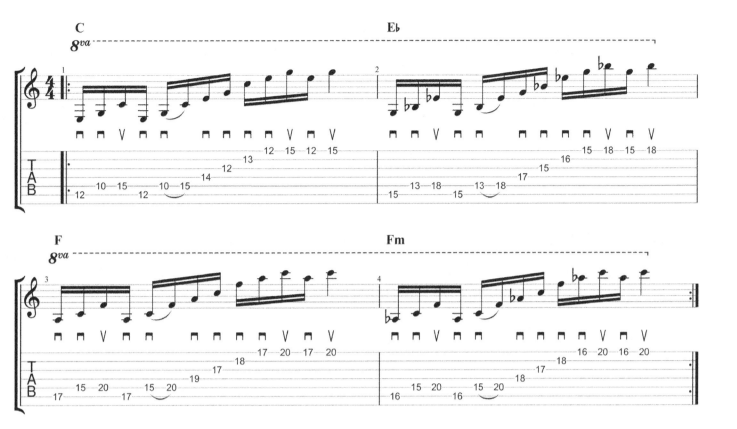

Example 3g uses the seven-string major and minor triads from Chapter Two in a chord progression consisting of A Major, B Minor, D Major and D Minor. The two major triads using the same staggered ascent from the low B string to high B string and then from the A string to the high E string. The minor triads use one pit stop on the way up before ascending through the whole seven-string shape.

Example 3g:

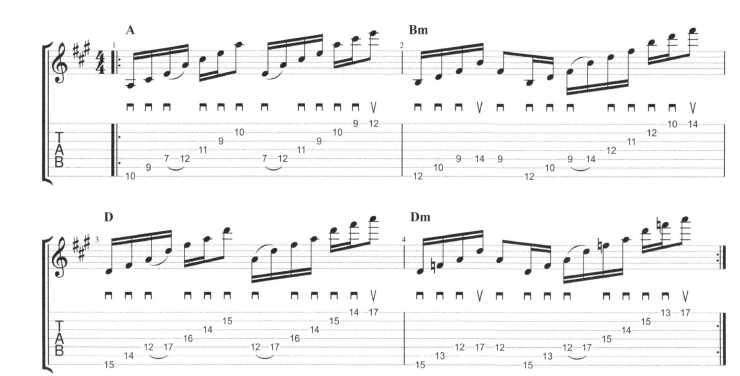

How to Practise Chapter Three

Since the picking hand requirements of these etudes each correspond to a development drill in Chapter Two, I suggest switching your focus to the musical applications and fingering hand requirements presented in this chapter. If you're confident enough with the material in the previous chapter, you might choose to replace it altogether with these etudes. If you feel you're not quite there yet, drill the appropriate exercise from Chapter Two as a warm-up for its linked etude in Chapter Three.

You could, for example, warm-up your picking hand with Example 2a from slow to EOA a couple of times, then run Example 3a through the three stages of development discussed in the conclusion of Chapter Two.

As soon as any exercise serves little to no developmental gain, replace it with one that is more advanced so that your practice time is not eaten up playing things you can already do (unless it's for enjoyment, of course). As your volume of practice material increases, your time may not. If you only have thirty to sixty minutes to practice, make it count with material that stretches you as a player.

Begin each practice session with a plan of what you'd like to achieve. Doing so is more likely to produce a feeling of accomplishment, even if you take just a few steps down a long road.

Chapter Four: Descending Strategy

In this section, shapes from Chapter Two will be used to build your descending sweep picking technique. Working in the opposite direction to the previous two chapters necessitates a few crucial changes to the method. The modified components of descending sweeping are:

- Upward (descending) sweep picking technique

- Upward rest stroke

- Upward pick slant with a couple of forced downward exceptions

- Inside turning mechanic, upscaping and downscaping

Sweeping in the upward direction feels slightly unnatural to many players at first, so don't be discouraged if your technique requires a little more attention in this area. Since picking with a downward slant is arguably the most common natural orientation among guitarists, creating a mirrored version of your technique can take time. Another potential hurdle in this endeavour stems from the fact that descending often involves alternating the pick slants at either end.

In isolation, upward sweep picking drills like Example 4a can be executed with an upward pick slant throughout, but in more realistic usage (like that of Example 4b) changes to the direction and pick slant will occur. In such cases, it's essential to keep the sweep as logical as possible and minimise the effect of the directional changes.

Example 4a:

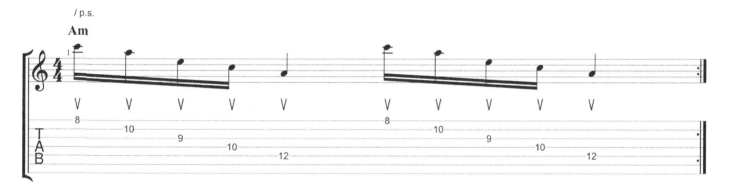

While many players will naturally head to the first note of Example 4b with a downward pick slant, downscaping needs to occur between the two notes on the high E string to set up the upward pick slant required for descending sweep picking. When arriving at the 12th fret of the A string via the rest stroke from the D string, upscaping occurs coming out of the A note to set up the necessary downward pick slant for the subsequent notes on the D and G strings, as well as the return to the high E string on repeats.

Example 4b:

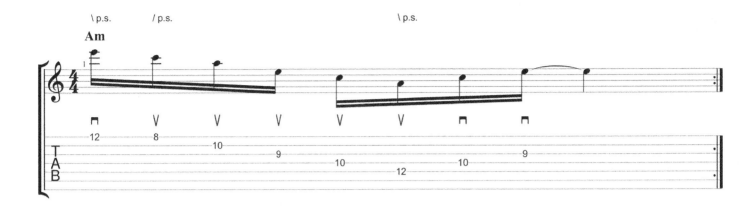

Set the two previous examples aside for the time being and progress through the following drills to incrementally develop the descending approach.

As a two-string drill, Example 4c contains only one sweep picking stroke. The primary objective is to become accustomed to the constant changes in pick slant. The first note of the loop occurs on a downstroke with downward pick slant, switching to an upward pick slant for the sweep back through the 8th fret of the high E string to the 10th fret of the B string.

After landing on the B string via the rest stroke, adjust into downward pick slant so that the pick is not caught between the B and G strings, and has clear passage back to the high E string. It is somewhat like flicking into downward pick slant out of the upstroke and will occur on whichever note is lowest as the triad expands across more strings.

On the first downstroke of bar one, the downward pick slant is not mandatory, but since it will be on the repeats, it has been indicated as such for continuity. The degree of pick slant does not need to be extreme in any of the examples, since exaggerated leaning can cost you time and energy. Enough slant to enable clean string changes without overt hopping is all that is necessary. At speed, the pick might even look neutral with this kind of pattern or create an illusion akin to a bending spoon trick. The pick slant changes will occur on the same notes each time.

Example 4c:

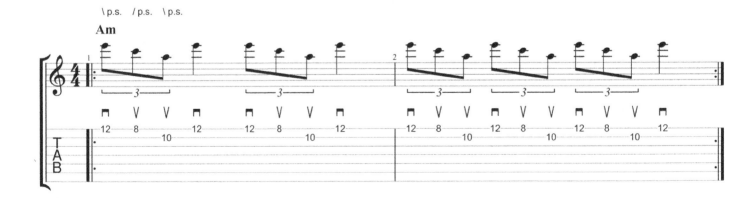

As the size of the triad is increased, the picking mechanic merely requires an extra upstroke and rest stroke per new string, shifting the inside turning mechanic to the final string before the turnaround. The larger the triad, the more you can take advantage of the directional flow of the notes, as Example 4d demonstrates.

Example 4d:

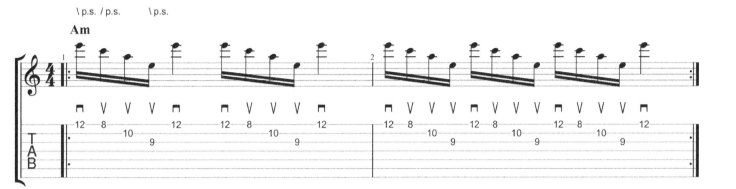

Permutations of the previous example do not change the placement of pick strokes and slants. Example 4e starts on an upstroke but is effectively the same pattern used in bar two of the last drill.

Example 4e:

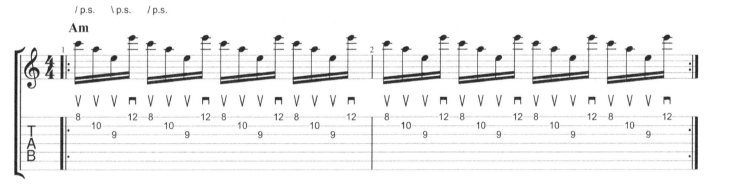

As Example 4f spans four strings, the directional flow of upward sweeping becomes more apparent. The rhythm of this example uses 1/16th and 1/8th notes so that speed and accuracy can be targeted within a single pattern.

Example 4f:

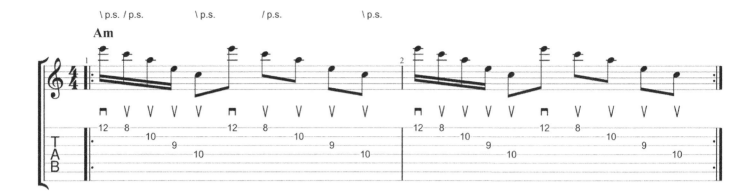

Approaching the two notes located on the A string, Example 4g uses all picked notes to maintain definition, whereas Example 4h uses a pull-off from the 12th fret to the 7th fret to allow flow as the pick continues in the upward direction to the low E string. It then ends with an inside turn back to the A string.

Example 4g:

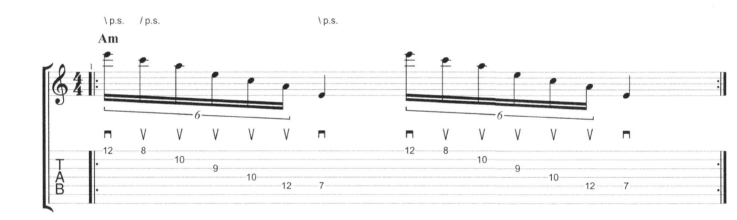

Example 4h:

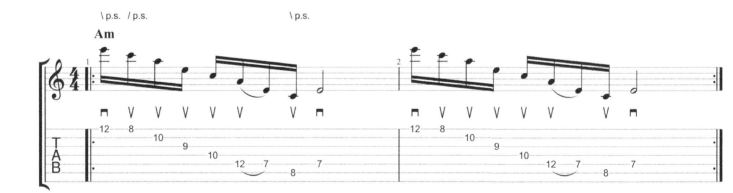

Descending across all seven strings simply delays the change in direction, and on which string the upscaping occurs. In bar two of Example 4i, a variation occurs in the form of an extra low E note on the 5th fret of the low B string. Since there is no change in direction at the end of this bar, the pick can remain in an upward slant until the end of the line.

Example 4i:

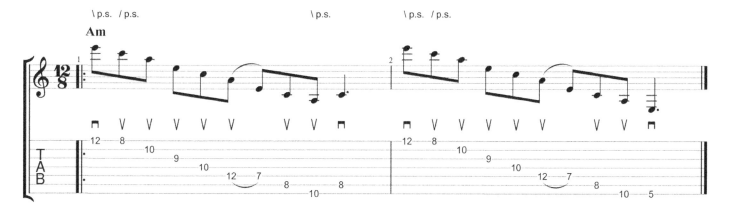

Before moving on to the descending etudes in Chapter Five, it's again recommended that you apply all the examples in this chapter to an A Major triad. It will be essential to weave together major and minor shapes with equal dexterity and, in the chapters that follow, to be as comfortable with descending sweeps as ascending sweeps.

How to Practise Chapter Four

If you're anything like me, more time might be spent in the cognitive stage of learning this descending technique than the ascending approach.

Your goal for this chapter is to perform descending sweeps with the same accuracy and confidence as their ascending counterparts. One way to track your progress during the associative stage is to play ascending and descending triads side by side within the same string groups. An example of this would be to alternate between Example 2m and Example 4h. Compare them in free time at first, then bring in the metronome for some analytical comparison.

As with the ascending approach, the descending approach will be applied musically in the etudes that follow.

Chapter Five: Descending Etudes

You should now have a sound knowledge of the implications and applications of pick slant in descending sweep picking. For that reason, pick slant indicators have been omitted from the following examples since they are the same as the descending drills in the previous chapter, e.g. the two-string exercises in Chapter Four use the same mechanics as two-string etudes in this chapter, and so on.

Example 5a is based on the picking of Example 4c but with six different triads across the four bars of the etude. Avoid letting position shifts affect your timing and work at speeds you can maintain all the way through before accelerating. To play the same etude two octaves lower, move everything to the low E and low B strings using the same frets.

Example 5a:

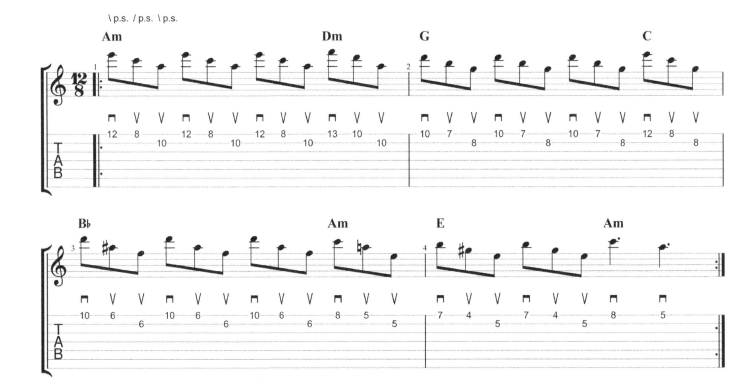

Example 5b is in 3/4 time and uses three-string minor and diminished triads and inversions. Alternate between clean and distorted tones as you practise etudes such as this, to ensure that your technique is clean and no string noise occurs.

While the diminished triads are named separately, each one functions harmonically as a dominant V chord (E7b9) to form a perfect cadence with the A Minor triad.

In the D Diminished triad (D F Ab) in bar three, the G# note is enharmonically equivalent to the Ab note in the triad. G# is used in the notation because it best represents the 7th degree of the A Harmonic Minor scale.

Example 5b:

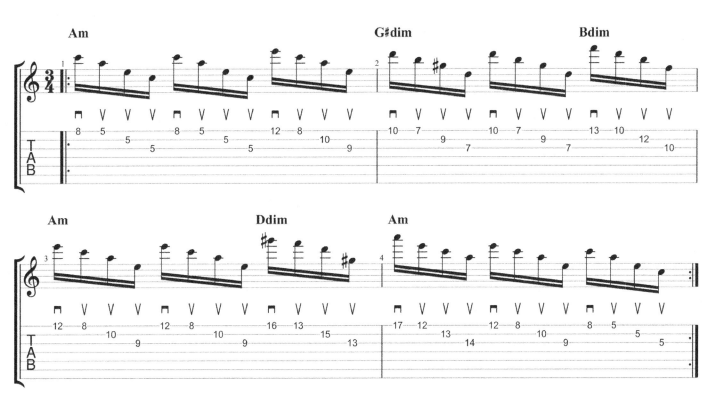

Example 5c uses major, minor and diminished triads. Since several of the triads start halfway through beats of the bar, take care to ensure that you execute them according to the rhythms and pick strokes indicated.

Example 5c:

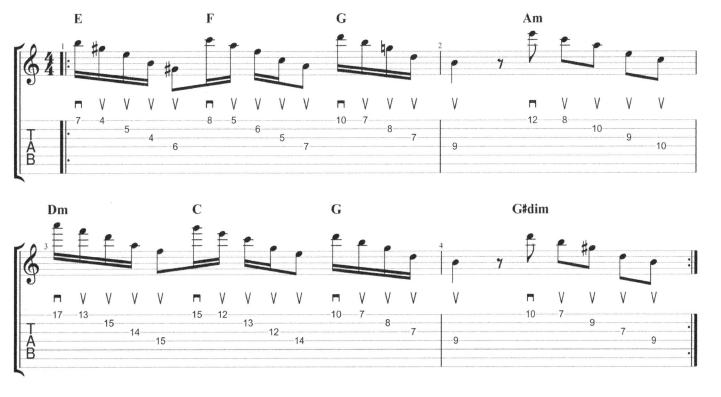

Example 5d uses a seven-string descending idea through four chords in the key of C Major. While the general direction is downward, the 3rd beat of each bar features a trill on the A string.

Example 5d:

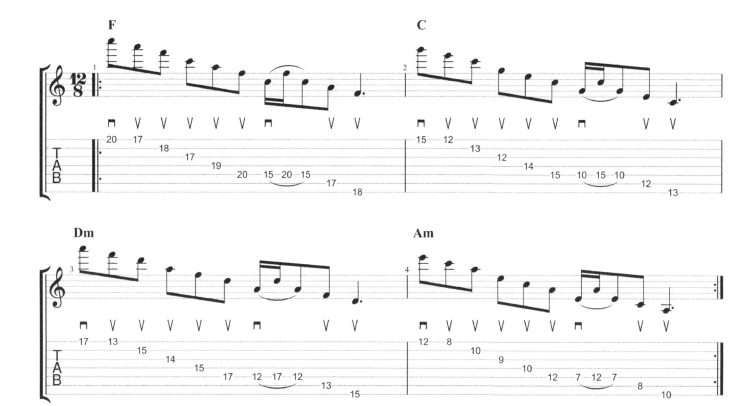

The final descending etude (Example 5e), is the most complicated example in the book so far and will test your ability to combine alternate picking and sweep picking with consistent timing and tidy execution. It uses all seven strings and passes through chords in the key of E Minor.

Example 5e:

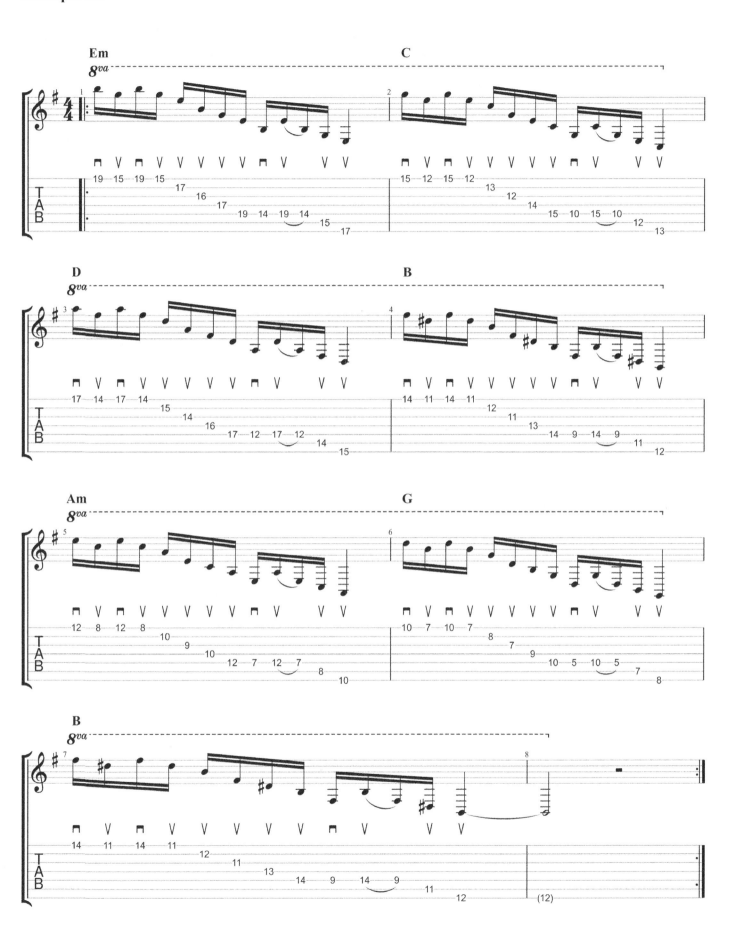

How to Practise Chapter Five

Your goals here are much the same as in Chapter Three: apply the mechanics in a musical way using the previous drills for development and warm-up purposes. You should recall the shapes quite easily by now, and an associative stage of mechanical development should allow for time to focus on where each upcoming arpeggio will be located on the fretboard.

Chapter Six: Bidirectional Strategies

Now that you have systemised ascending and descending sweep picking in isolation, it's time to combine them and consider some options that arise from directional changes. The bidirectional strategies allow for a lot of personalisation.

Mechanics used in this section include:

- Double and single turnarounds

- Downward and upward sweep picking technique

- Rest strokes in both directions

- Alternating pick slant

- Inside and outside turning mechanics (upscaping and downscaping)

- Hammer-ons and pull-offs

Double Turnarounds

When an ascending picking form is combined with its equal but opposite descent, it produces something I call the *Double Turnaround*. The term refers to the use of repeated notes at either end of a triad, so that both sweep directions begin on down strokes, as shown in the next three drills.

Each triad uses an even number of pick strokes to change direction, regardless of how many single-note strings appear between the turnaround points. With swift direction changes, it's important to remember that changes to pick slant can occur slightly before or after the points noted. Changes that are too forced and abrupt might even impact your potential speed.

If it flows and you're avoiding getting the pick stuck between strings, you're doing it right!

Example 6a:

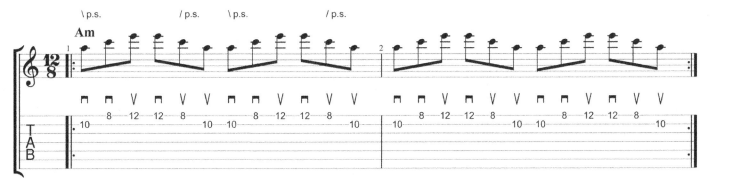

Example 6b:

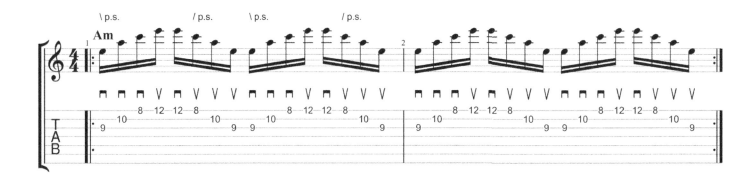

Example 6c:

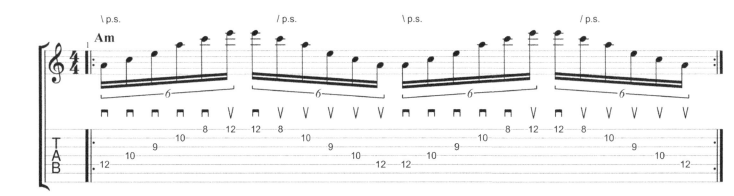

Example 6d:

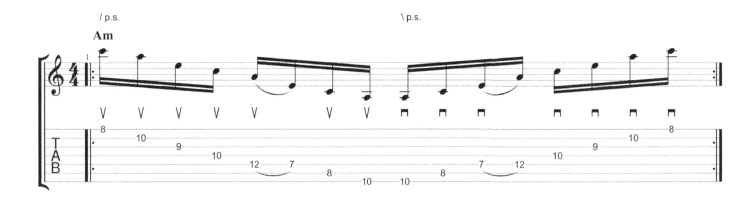

To avoid repeating the same pitch at either end of a double turnaround sweep, the picking mechanics can be applied to progressions of triads that change after each ascent or descent. Examples 6e to 6h correspond to the two-, three-, five- and seven-string triad forms with a four-chord progression applied.

42

Example 6e:

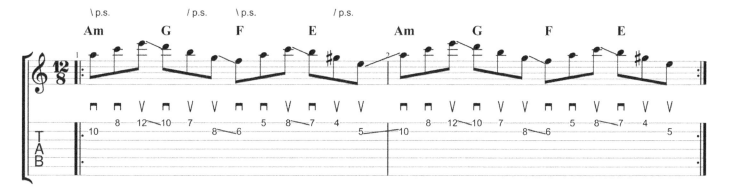

Example 6f:

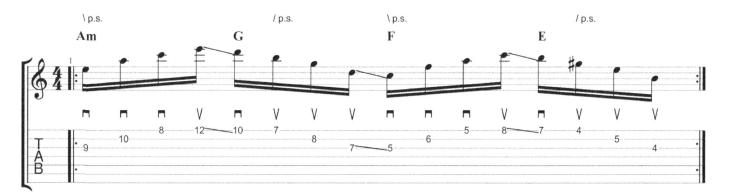

Example 6g:

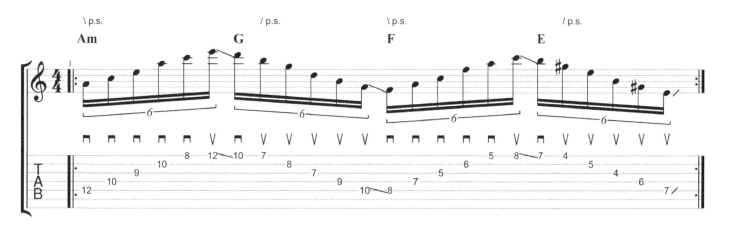

Example 6h:

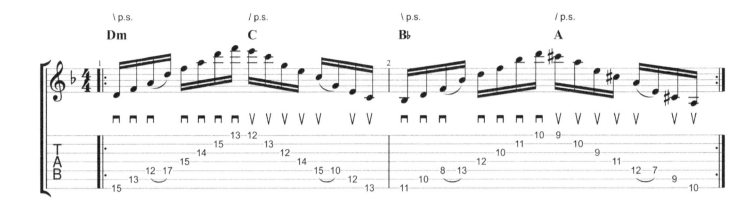

Single Turnarounds

Looping a sweep picking pattern without duplicating the top or bottom notes is called a *single turnaround*. The highest or lowest note is not played twice merely for ease of changing direction, and the turnaround does not require an even number of notes.

The extended five-string D Minor triad in Example 6i works as a single turnaround lick. The pick strokes used in beats 1 and 2 naturally reoccur on the repeat of the phrase in beats 3 and 4. The ease of repetition undoubtedly accounts for the frequent use of this sweeping form by many players.

Example 6i:

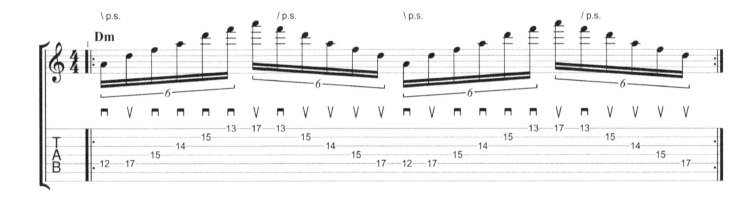

With the addition of a hammer-on in the ascent and a pull-off in the descent for a smoother ride, this form works even better. Example 6j offers an etude for this approach using D Minor and C Major triads. With only two picked notes on the high E string, it makes sense to adjust the pick slant coming out of the ascending half of each arpeggio and into the descending half.

Example 6j:

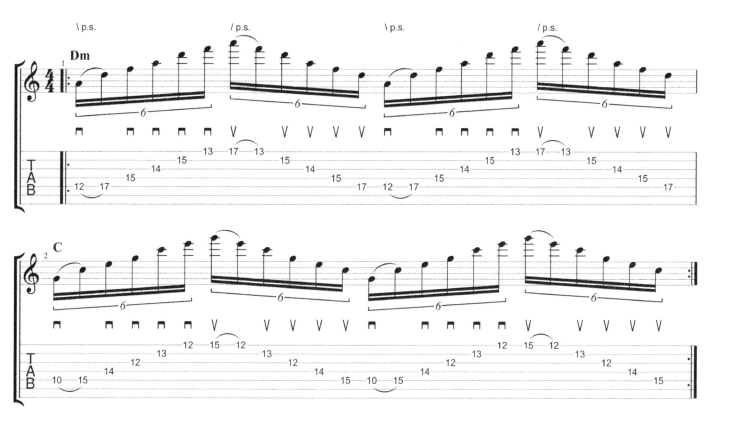

Seven-string forms can also benefit from the turnaround advantages of two notes on a string at either end of a triad. In Example 6k, let's add an A note to the 10th fret of the low B string. Starting with an upward sweep from the A string to the low B string and using the extra low note, the turnaround aspects of this lick have a similar feel to the five-string counterpart in the previous example.

Example 6k:

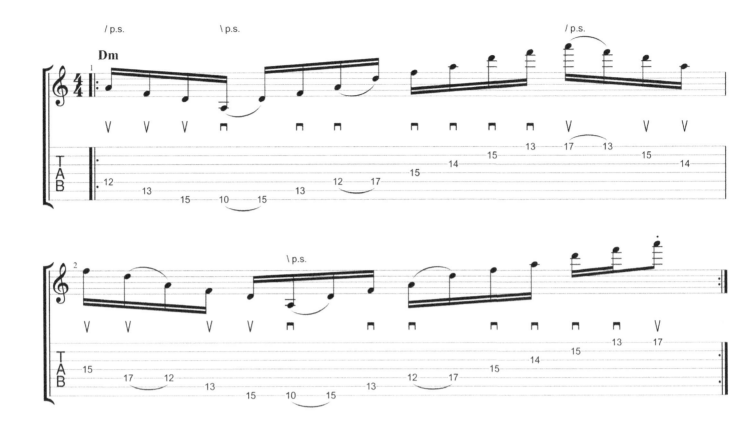

Groups where the lowest string of each shape contains only a single note can be less intuitive than previous examples, raising questions about inside picking versus outside picking, and using one set of mechanics the first time versus a different version on the repeats. Some patterns may also create confusion due to unique approaches used by various famous sweep pickers. Let's demystify that.

To strategise your personal approach and remove all uncertainty from the options, let's run through the string groups progressively.

Two-string Single Turnarounds

Ascending and descending within the two-string A Minor triad presents a problem early on if all notes are picked. Evident in Example 6l, an ascending sweep only occurs the first time since the drill is soon forced into an inside alternate picking form upon repeating.

Example 6l:

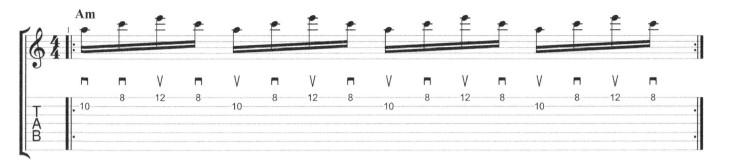

The most straightforward remedy is to maintain the downward pick slant of the ascending approach in Chapter Two and use a pull-off between the E and C notes on the high E string. Doing so facilitates endless repeats of the pattern without changes to pick strokes or pick slant and ensures no more than two picked notes on the turnaround string.

Example 6m:

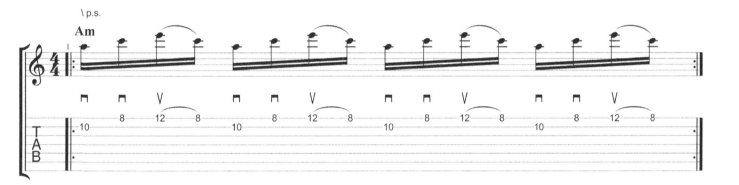

Starting the loop from a different point still requires no change to pick strokes or slant. The sweep just occurs at the end of each beat instead of the beginning.

Example 6n:

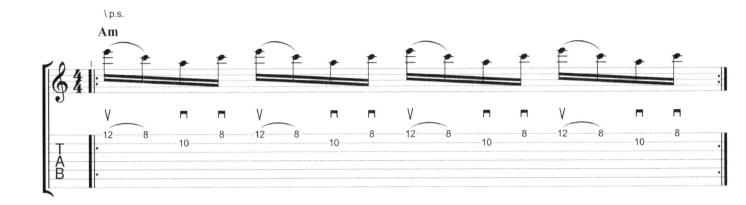

Extending Single Turnarounds to All Strings

Limiting the number of picked notes on the high E string to two helps form a smooth looping strategy for larger string groups. *Down, up, pull-off* will be the go-to approach for single turnaround triads unless you specifically desire the effect of picking every note.

Expanding Example 6m to ascending three-, four- and five-string groups is simple. Add a new lower string each time, with another downstroke and rest stroke for each.

Example 6o:

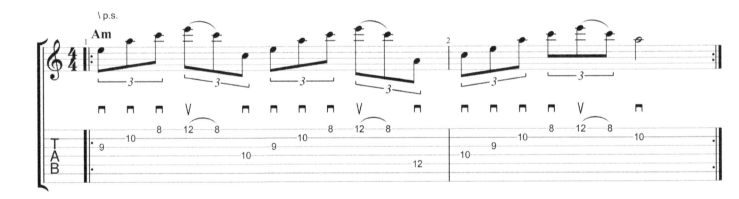

Let's deal with single notes at the bottom of triads next. In the following line, should the C note (10th fret on the D string) in beat 3 of the first bar be played as a continuation of the upward sweep from beat 2, or with a downstroke as the beginning of a new ascending sweep?

Example 6p:

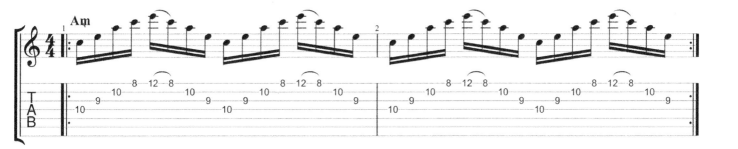

Like the glass half empty / half full scenario, the truth is that it depends on how you look at it.

Example 6p2 treats the C as part of the descending upstroke sweep at the beginning of the 3rd beat of bar one. Note that pick slant changes coming out of the C note in preparation for the inside turn mechanic that begins the next ascending downstroke sweep.

Example 6p2:

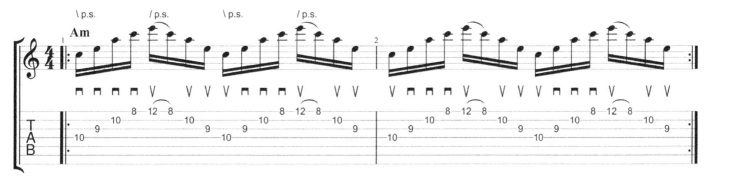

Example 6p3 presents the other option whereby each C note on the D string is considered the start of a new ascending downstroke sweep. For the outside turn mechanic to work, the pick slant needs to change coming out of the E note on the 9th fret of the G string before each repeat.

Example 6p3:

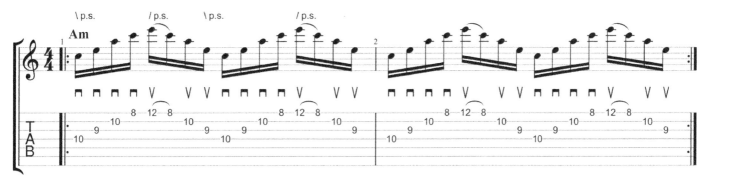

It's OK to choose one or work at mastering both. Examine the approaches, choose the option you prefer for the situation and apply the pick slant changes suited to your choice.

Example 6q applies an inside turnaround to the lowest point of six-string and seven-string patterns. You can try this with an outside string change by switching the lowest note of each bar to downstrokes. At the high E string turnaround in bar one, beat 4, changes occur to the picking execution and pick slant by repeating the descent across the bar line.

Example 6q:

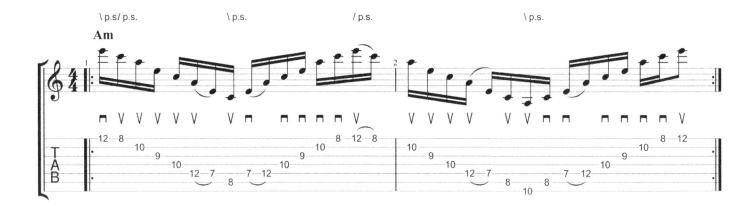

In Example 6r, the three-string portions in the first half of bar one and the last half of bar two are typical of players like Yngwie Malmsteen. The G-string here is treated as part of an ascending sweep using a downstroke, requiring an outside turn mechanic from the B string. The lick begins with an upstroke since that's what will occur with repeats coming out of the last sweep of bar two.

Example 6r:

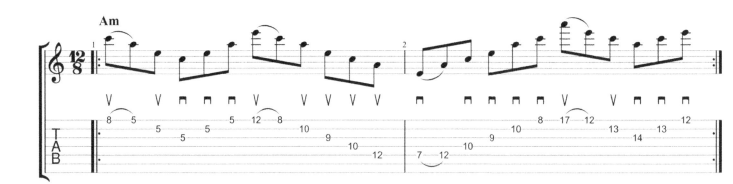

Try also using an upstroke and inside turn mechanic from the B string to the G string in both bars of the previous example. In Malmsteen's case, the outward downstroke on turnarounds is the go-to approach for just about any sweep picking line.

Mid-air Changes in Direction

To get musically creative with bidirectional sweeping, you can change direction at any point within a triad instead of waiting to arrive at the top or bottom of a range of notes. The next couple of examples mimic the effect that a harpist or pianist would create when cascading through arpeggios.

Example 6s begins on the lowest C note of an A Minor triad, cascading back and forth as it reaches new turning points throughout. The inside turning mechanic is the one most frequently used in this example, so take care regarding timing and pick slant.

Coming into the 2nd beat of bar one, I've opted for outside picking from the A string back to the low E string to remain in a downward pick slant until the turnaround point in beat 3.

Example 6s:

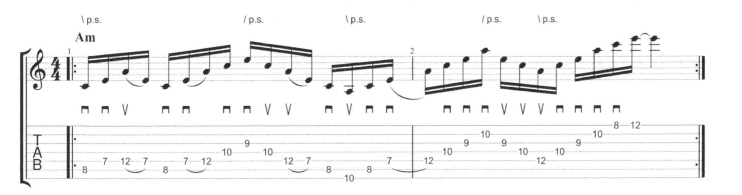

Example 6t contains even more single turnarounds with inside picking, aided by upscaping and downscaping to avoid getting the pick trapped between strings. The pick strokes reflect a true economy picker's approach using the most directional string changes available. Try bar one of this exercise as a standalone drill to focus on all those changes to pick slant and direction and keep your slant changes subtle to make the directional changes efficient and swift.

Example 6t:

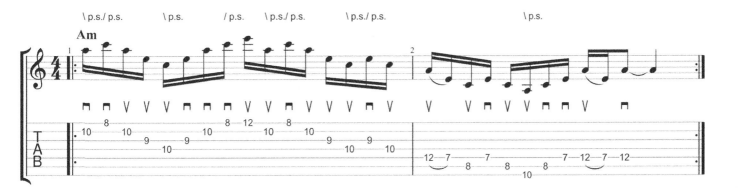

When you've spent some time developing fluency with the last two examples, try throwing in spontaneous string and direction changes to break out of straight up and down arpeggio playing in improvisation.

How to Practise Chapter Six

In most cases where things can be done in multiple ways, I tell those who study with me to *put it through the speed test*. What immediately feels best in the cognitive stage of learning might not always be the method that advances to the autonomous stage.

For a time, you may have to let competing strategies do battle during your practice time, assessing the benefits and applications of each until one stands out as a true preference, capable of helping you deliver your ideas at the desired tempo. To that end, try directional changes in all the ways discussed in this chapter, eventually putting the most energy into the choices that produce the most results.

With the bidirectional etudes that follow in Chapter Eight, you will have many chances to put all the sweeping chops you've acquired to use in examples that most reflect *real-world* usage of technique.

Chapter Seven: Bidirectional Etudes

Since Chapter Six outlines various options for two-way sweep picking, each etude in this chapter will reference a related mechanical approach from the previous section. Example 7a is built around a *circle of fourths* chord progression typical of baroque-influenced rock. The single turnaround picking mechanic from Example 6k is used throughout. You can move this etude down to the sixth and seventh strings using the same frets to play it two octaves lower.

Example 7a:

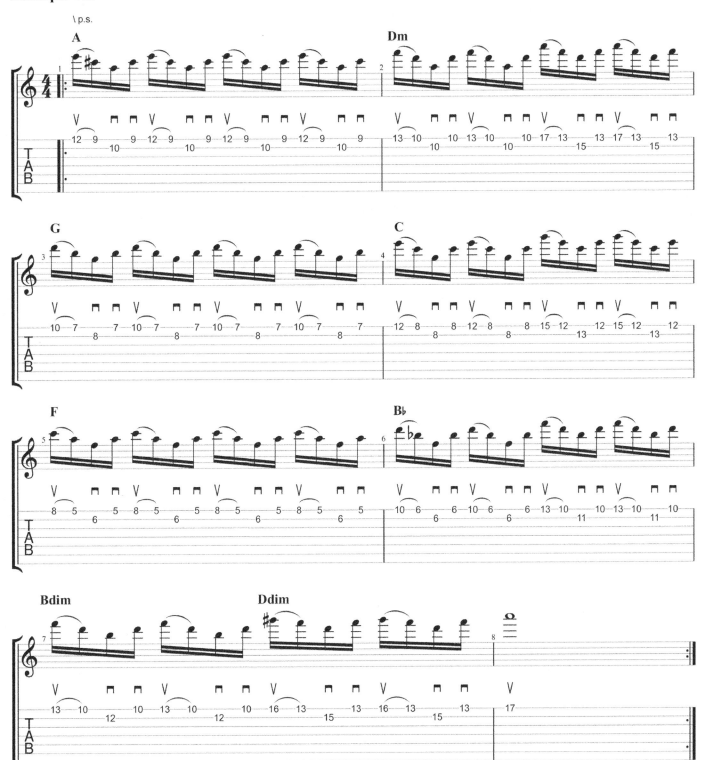

Example 7b uses the double turnaround mechanic from Example 6a on the D and G strings in a progression sourced from the key of G Major. Bars one and two ascend and descend within each position before changing triads, while bars three and four split up the picking mechanic between ascending and descending triads.

Example 7b:

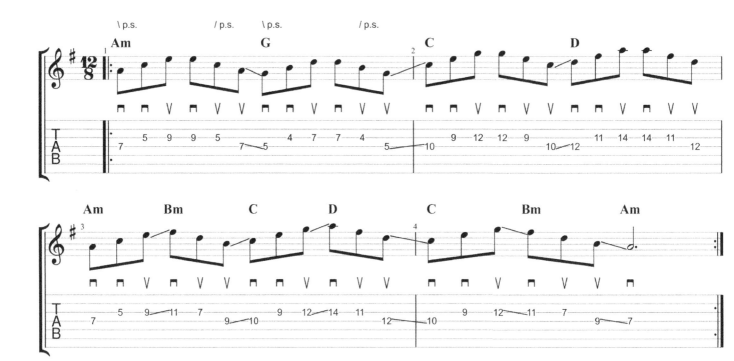

With the same harmonic progression as the previous etude, Example 7c is written for three string triads with double turnarounds throughout.

Example 7c:

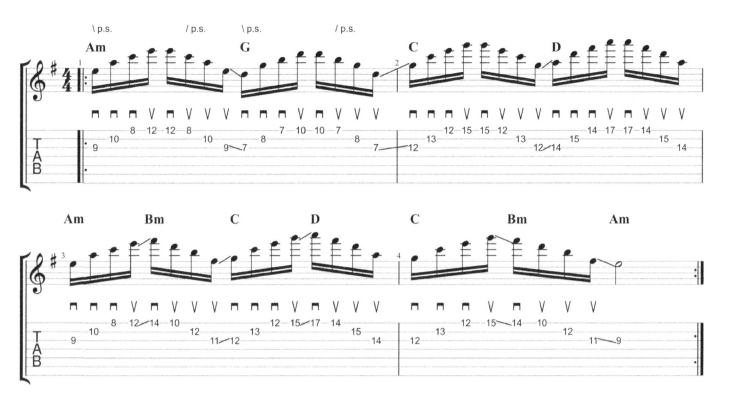

Built with the inside turn mechanic and alternating pick slants, the next etude expands and contracts within each triad, using three, five and four strings for each chord in the progression. Practise each bar separately at first, reconnecting the parts when you've memorised all four shapes. Ensure that your transitions are in time with the beat when putting it back together.

Example 7d:

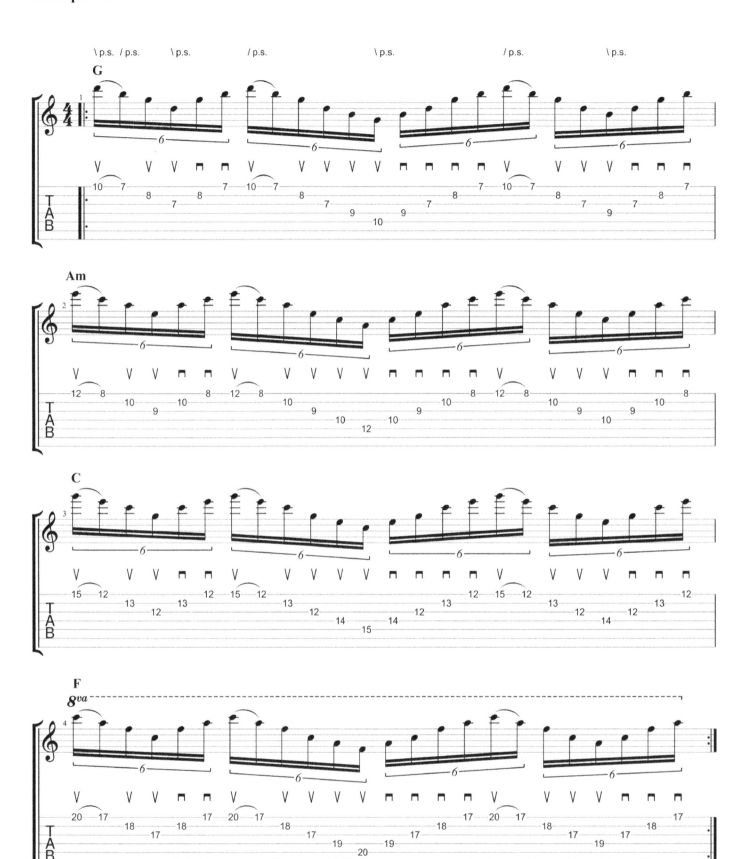

In Example 7e, the A triad in bar one and the C triad in bar three use the same shape, direction changes and pick slant application. While bar two stays within the A Major triad of the previous measure, bar four switches to a D Major triad starting from the second 1/8th note of beat 1, which finishes on the D root note at the end of beat 3.

Example 7e:

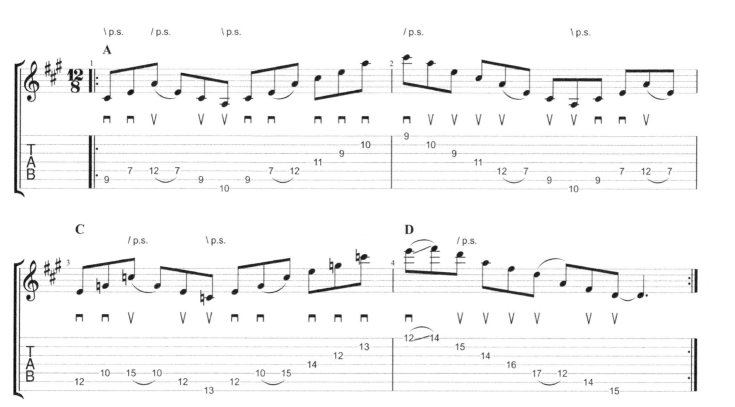

To complete the chapter, Example 7f is designed to work the inside turn mechanic at several points within one triad. Timing is crucial as you switch between 1/16th notes and 1/16th note triplets, with direction changes occurring on most strings at various points. When you can play this example, apply the sequence used to other chord progressions.

Example 7f:

How to Practise Chapter Seven

Moving forward, it's vital that you take the ideas presented in these etudes and make them your own with different chord progressions, styles, phrasing and tempi.

Having studied all that you have so far, you'll probably notice that etudes like the ones in this chapter become associative and autonomous quicker than the drills from which they are derived. This is because your motor skills are recognising the application of standard moves. As time passes, you will find new material even more natural to develop, allowing more emphasis on the musical delivery of your sweep picking lines.

Your focus in this chapter (besides playing neatly and in time) is to enjoy the music. Hopefully, the journey is enjoyable already, but with some much cooler material up your sleeve, the joy factor increases as you make actual music, taking you a level above merely *getting it right*.

Recommendations for further study

Here are some pieces to seek out to put your bidirectional sweep picking chops to use in music.

- *Altitudes* – Jason Becker

- *Serrana* – Jason Becker

- *Race with Destiny* – Vinnie Moore

- *Demon Driver* – Yngwie Malmsteen

- *Overture* – Yngwie Malmsteen

- *Liar* – Yngwie Malmsteen

- *No Boundaries* – Michael Angelo Batio

- *Requiem for the Living* – Jeff Loomis

Chapter Eight: Fretboard Coverage - Triads

With the mechanics of ascending, descending and bidirectional sweep picking at your disposal, it's time to expand the vocabulary of triads and arpeggios using various systems for fretboard coverage. With so many chord tones available across the neck, it's essential to examine the best ways to structure the options into manageable chunks that allow you to make music. To that end, this gargantuan chapter delves into the following:

• CAGED system Major triads

• Speed shape triads

• Major, Minor, Diminished and Augmented triad mapping

• Suspended 2nd and Suspended 4th arpeggio mapping

CAGED Shapes Versus Speed Shapes

Many guitarists learn the location of chord tones within the CAGED system, a method of visualising and zoning the fretboard according to the open chord shapes of C Major, A Major, G Major, E Major and D Major and the location of the root notes of each.

While valuable for improvisation and the integration of scales and chord tones, the tonal overlap and irregular layouts mean that this system of coverage might not provide the mechanical consistency one expects for a technique like sweep picking. However, understanding the use of triads within the CAGED system will help you understand the refinements that are used in the *speed shape* approach.

The following five patterns highlight the A Major triad notes (A, C#, E) within the seven-string extensions of the common six-string CAGED scale patterns in the key of A Major. I've displayed these starting with the E Shape since many of us learned our first *old faithful* major scale shape within this pattern.

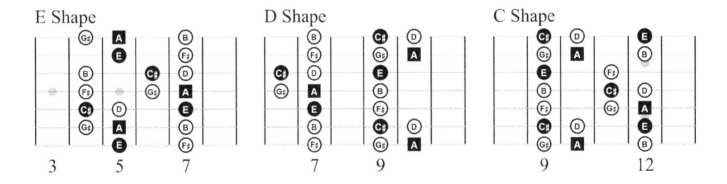

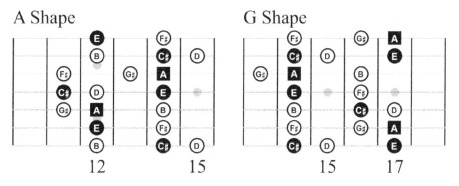

A Shape   G Shape

12   15   15   17

Fast arpeggio lines are often aided by systemised fingerings and picking templates that can be applied to a variety of chords and inversions – something that CAGED shapes don't always offer. By eliminating some of the positional and tonal overlaps of the CAGED patterns and tweaking the layout so that identical picking forms can be applied, the *Speed Shapes* cover the horizontal fretboard space in just three patterns – one shape per chord tone. The three patterns connect any number of strings for extensive fretboard coverage and can be modified for each chord type.

Speed Shapes for Major Triads - 1, 3, 5

In the six-string version of this book, I presented three shapes known as Speed Shapes 1, 2 and 3 based on hybrids of neighbouring CAGED shapes (E/D, D/C and A/G).

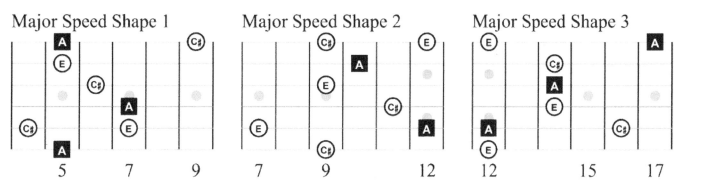

Major Speed Shape 1   Major Speed Shape 2   Major Speed Shape 3

5   7   9   7   9   12   12   15   17

To avoid confusion when migrating from six to seven strings or vice versa, let's keep the shape names the same. If it helps you remember which is which, Speed Shape 1 has a root note on the first string, Speed Shape 2 has the same root note on the second string and Speed Shape 3 has the same root note again on the third string.

Shape 2 has been the most frequently used pattern in the book so far and offers a very convenient layout requiring no finger rolling.

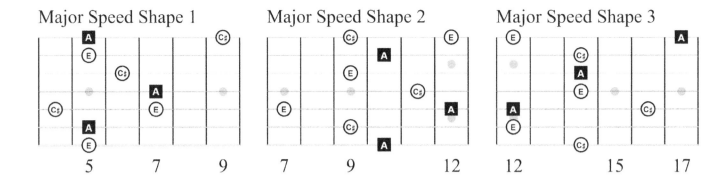

Major Speed Shape 1 Major Speed Shape 2 Major Speed Shape 3

Each shape is an inversion of the adjacent shapes in either direction, played using a number system layout of 1-1-2-1-1-1-2, referring to how many notes appear on each string from low B string to the high E. All the drills used in Chapters Two, Four and Six can be applied to each of these speed shapes without altering the picking patterns.

My suggested fingerings and execution for the A Major speed shapes are offered in Example 8a. Bars one and seven both feature the first Speed Shape but, in the higher octave, I use a second finger roll to fret the first two notes instead of the index/middle switcheroo of the lower pattern.

Example 8a – Major triad speed shapes across seven strings:

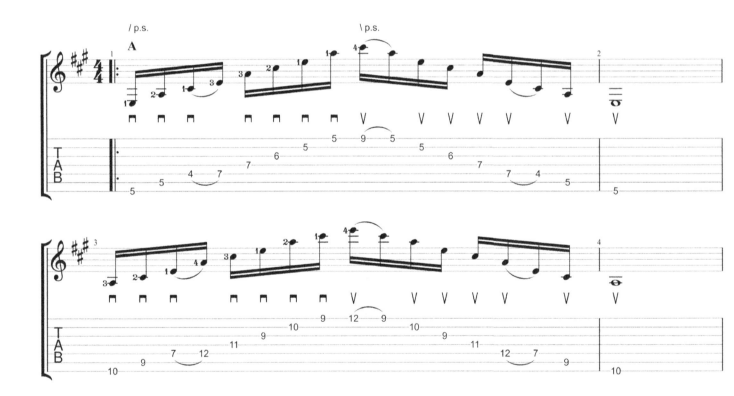

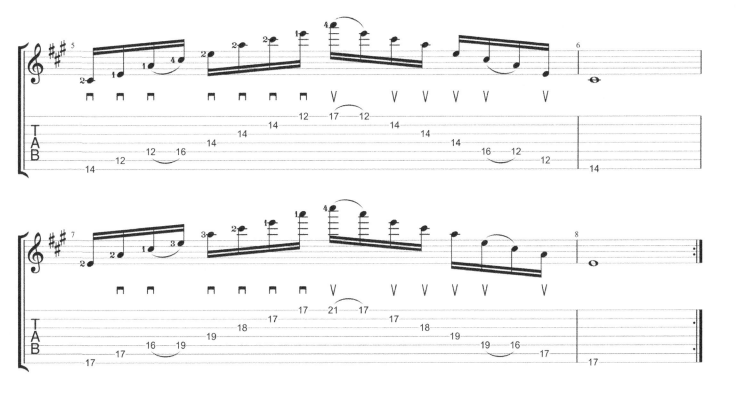

As we remove a string each time through Examples 8b to 8f, the fingering and picking remain the same as they pertain to each portion of the full pattern. I use various rhythms in these examples to fit the notes into bars of 4/4 time, so be sure to listen to the audio for rhythmic cues.

Example 8b - Major triad speed shapes across six strings:

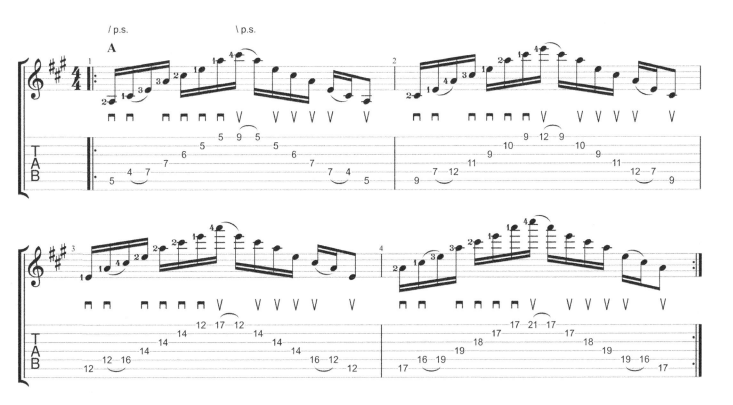

Example 8c – Major triad speed shapes across five strings:

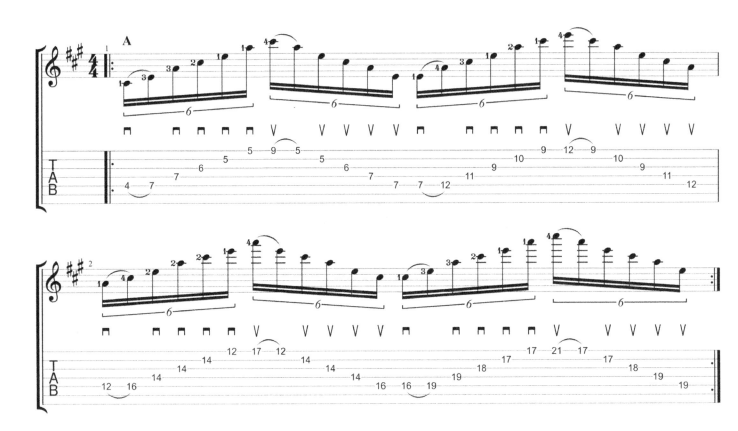

Example 8d – Major triad speed shapes across four strings:

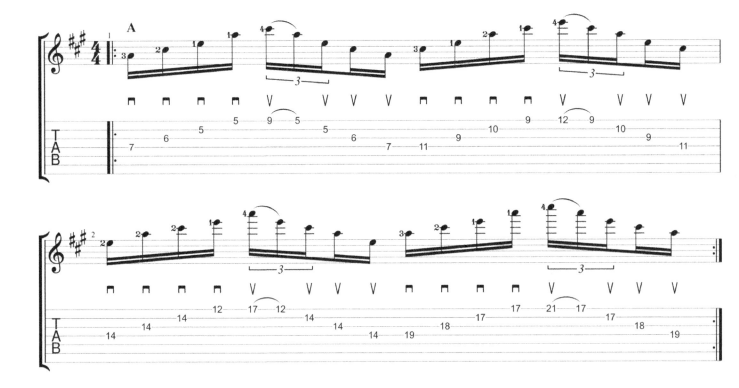

Example 8e – Major triad speed shapes across three strings:

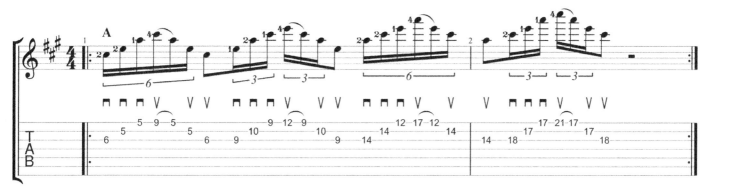

Example 8f – Major triad speed shapes across two strings:

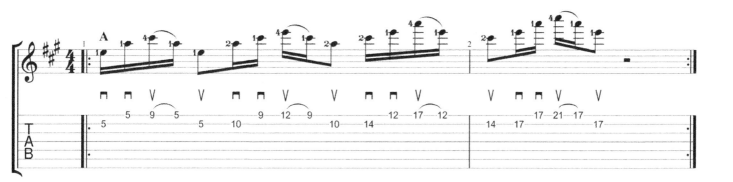

Using a mix of directions across whole and partial patterns can make for an exciting and seemingly endless flow of chord tones. Example 8g creates such an effect as it connects the three shapes of A Major.

Example 8g:

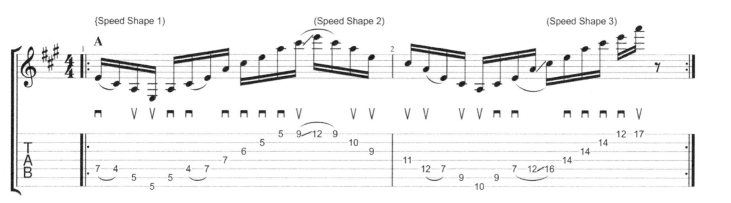

Shape Your Own Path

Any time a shape comes along that isn't to your liking, creating alternatives is just a matter of consulting the fretboard map for the chord in question, relocating notes with problematic fingerings or forming new patterns from scratch.

A Major triad across the fretboard

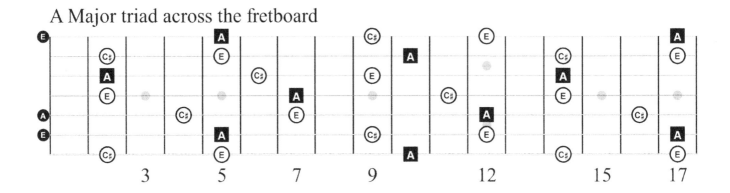

Speed Shapes for Minor Triads - 1, b3, 5

The transition from major to minor triads involves merely lowering the 3rd of the former by one semitone within each 1-1-2-1-1-1-2 picking form, producing the following shapes:

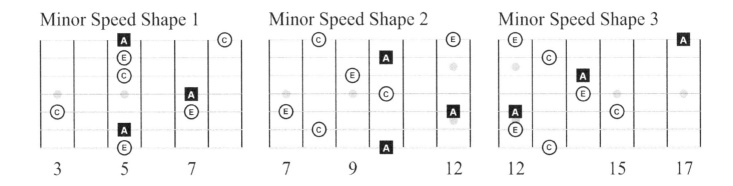

My suggested fingerings for the minor speed shapes (and any part thereof) are detailed in Example 8h. If you develop an alternative approach, ensure that your choices allow for fluid, accurate and consistent execution.

Example 8h:

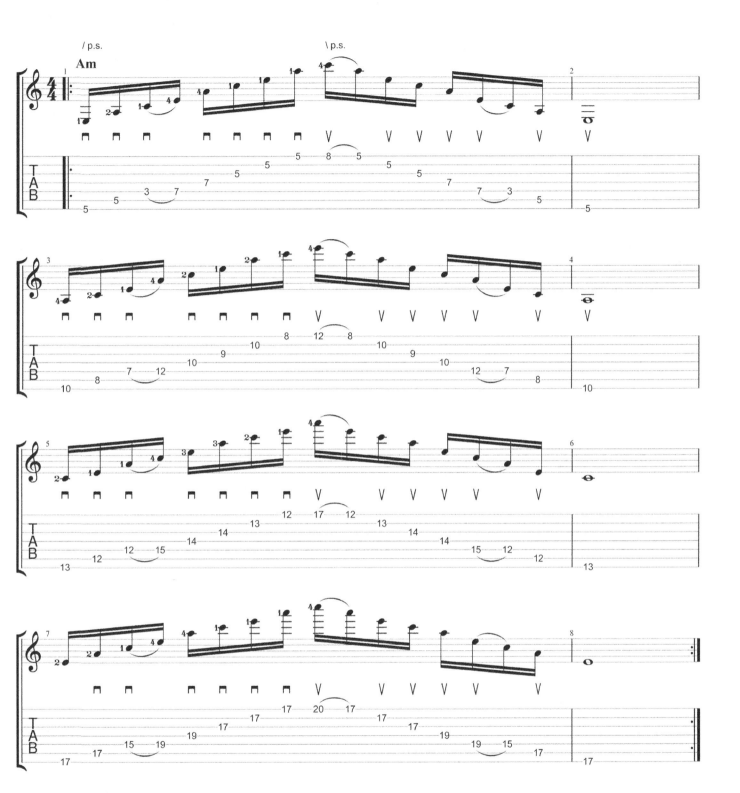

After learning the minor speed shapes, repeat Examples 8b to 8f using minor triads. Consult the fretboard map for minor triads if you wish to create alternative shapes.

A Minor triad across the fretboard

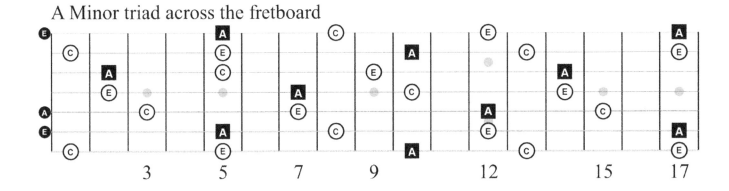

Progressions with Moving Shapes Versus Positional Shapes

Sweeping through chord progressions can be done with a very useful *voice-leading* approach by selecting shapes that occupy similar regions of the fretboard. Consider examples 8i and 8j, which compare position-jumping and voice-leading approaches. In Example 8i, the chords D Major, A Major, E Major and F# Minor use the same block sourced from Speed Shape 2.

Example 8i:

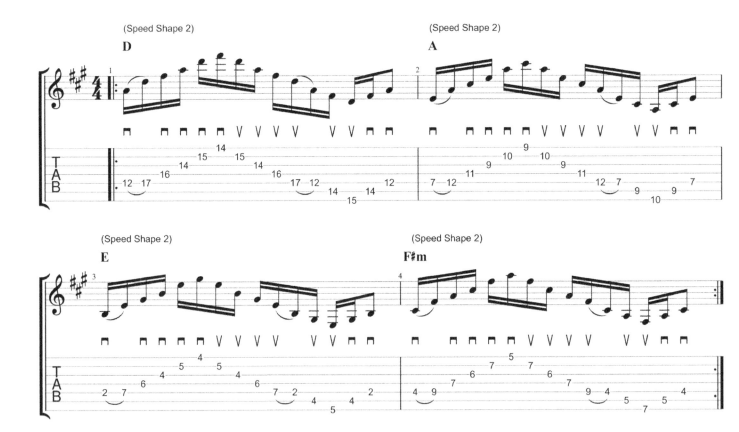

The wide position shifts and melodic intervals between each triad in the previous example can sound a little disjointed, even when executed perfectly. Example 8j counters that problem by using shapes that lead pleasantly into each new arpeggio. By using Speed Shape 2 of the D triad, Speed Shape 3 for the A triad, Speed Shape 1 for the E and Speed Shape 3 for the F#m, the intervals joining each chord change are much smaller.

Example 8j:

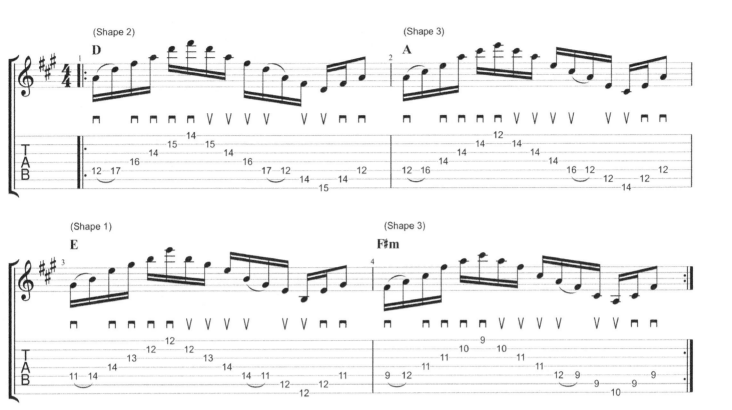

Example 8k provides yet another option for the same sequence of chords. Following a progression within a region of the neck is a great way to create unity and movement simultaneously.

Example 8k:

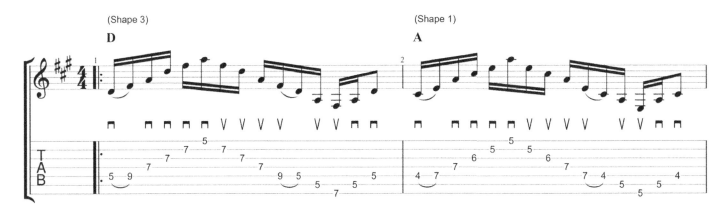

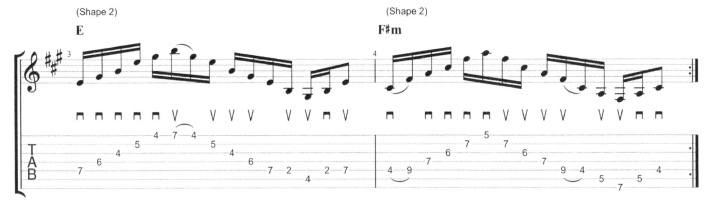

Speed Shapes for Augmented Triads – 1, 3, #5

The augmented triad evokes a mysterious sound with its construction of root note, major 3rd and augmented (raised) 5th intervals. Occurring naturally from the III degree of the harmonised *harmonic minor* and *melodic minor* scales and from each degree of the *whole tone scale*, augmented triads can be found by modifying major triad shapes. The result is a single shape that occurs in three locations because the chord consists of consecutive major 3rds.

The symmetrical construction of augmented triads means that Aaug, C#aug and E#aug (Faug, enharmonically) are not only chords unto themselves, but inversions of each other.

Due to the construction formula of the augmented triad (1, 3, #5), it's correct to refer to the 5th of Aaug as E# rather than F.

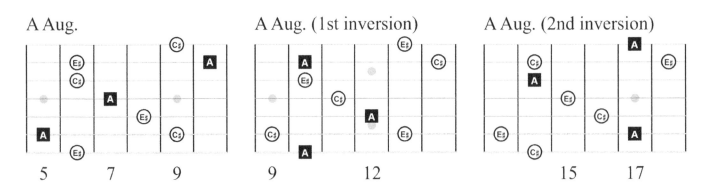

Inside the seven-string augmented pattern is a cool five-string shape from the low E string to the high B string. The number of notes in the shape make it perfect for sextuplet sweep licks like Example 8l, which demonstrates the convenience of moving a single shape around the fretboard. At high speed, it's a real attention-grabber!

Example 8l:

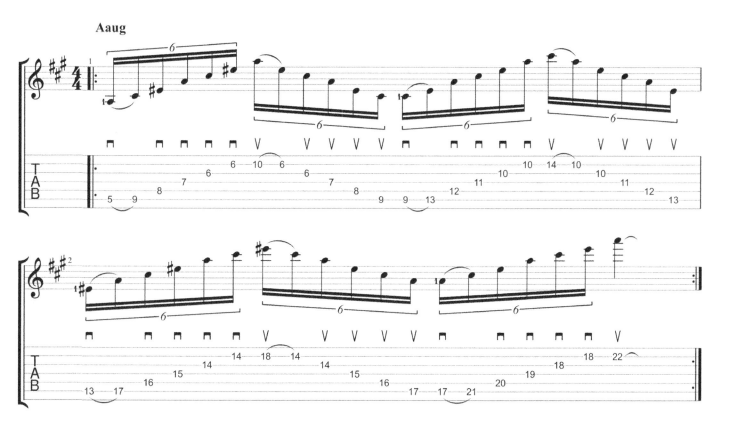

The fretboard map of an augmented triad reveals other possibilities for movable fingerings. See what shapes you can construct from the following diagram and work your ideas through interval jumps of major 3rds.

A Augmented triad across the fretboard

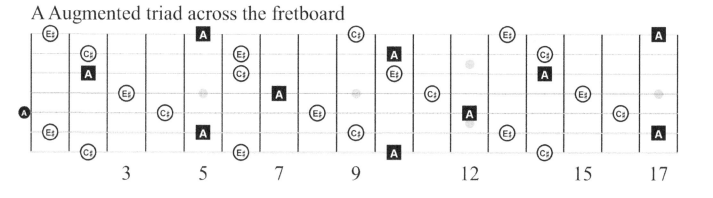

Example 8m takes advantage of a four-finger diagonal shape occurring from the low B string to the D string and the low E string to G string.

Example 8m:

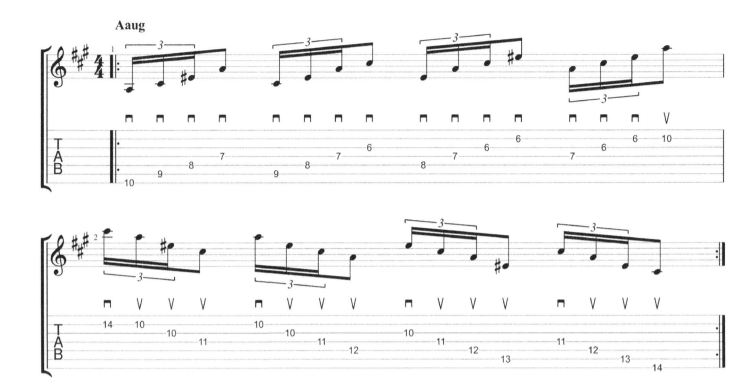

Using a repeated eight-note picking form and ascending in major 3rds, Example 8n climbs through string groups while descending in fretboard position each time. The first three units of eight use the same fingering shape on their respective string groups but are modified in bar two to stay faithful to the augmented triad.

Example 8n:

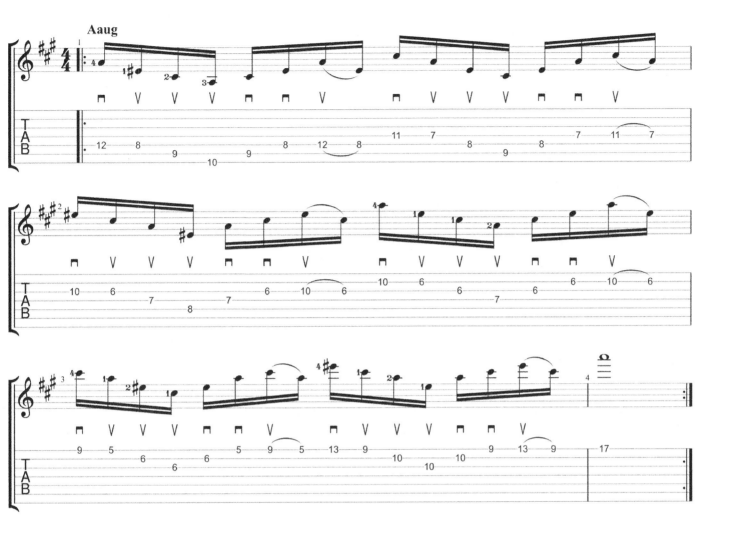

Example 8o switches from an A Major triad in bar one to an A Augmented triad in bar two. When repeating the drill, be sure to begin the A triad in bar one with your third finger each time.

Example 8o:

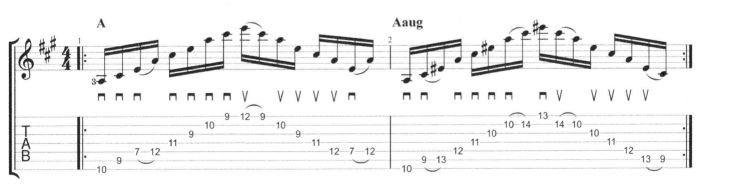

Speed Shapes for Diminished Triads – 1, b3, b5

Unlike the major 3rd stacks used to create an evenly-spaced augmented triad, diminished triads include an extra-large interval of six semitones from the b5 degree up to the next root note. The increased intervallic distance has an impact on the fretting hand layout where 5ths and roots previously lined up nicely on most string pairs in major and minor shapes.

A Diminished triad across the fretboard

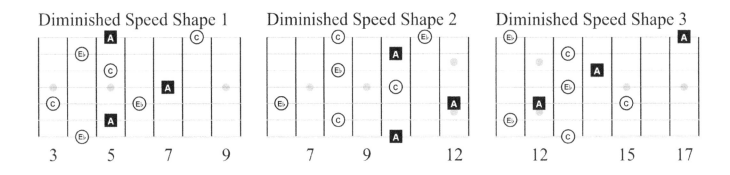

Converting minor triad speed shapes to diminished shapes by lowering all occurrences of the 5th sounds like a reasonable proposition, but the results are a bit of a stretch – literally!

Diminished Speed Shape 1   Diminished Speed Shape 2   Diminished Speed Shape 3

Speed Shape 2 is quite a useful shape depending on how high or low you find yourself on the fretboard for stretching purposes, but another approach that works in all three shapes is selective omission.

Since each of the shapes contain nine notes and there are only three different notes in a triad, selective omission is about removing a couple of technical hurdles in favour of executing something more practical to represent the desired sound. Here are three one-note-per-string variations I've come up with, as notated in Example 8p.

Diminished Omission 1   Diminished Omission 2   Diminished Omission 3

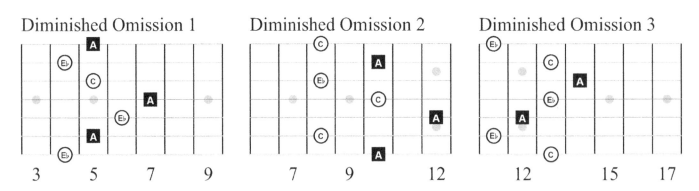

Example 8p:

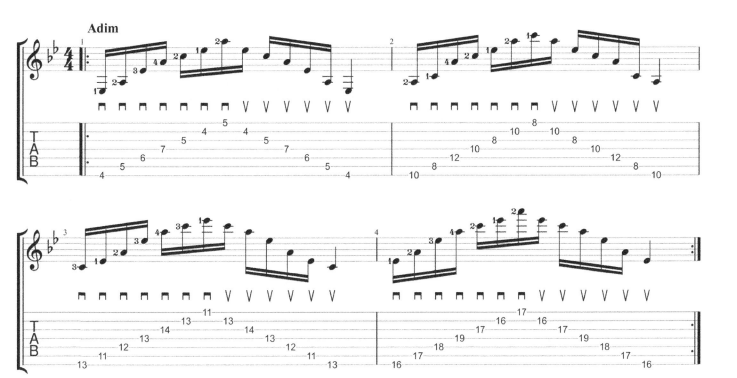

By consulting the fretboard for other possibilities, you can also find shapes like this string-skipping alternative. Example 8q starts with a Paul Gilbert-style string skipping sequence before descending in a one-note-per-string omission shape.

Omission 1 Alternative

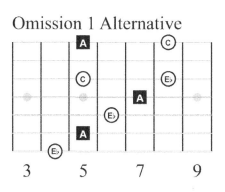

Example 8q:

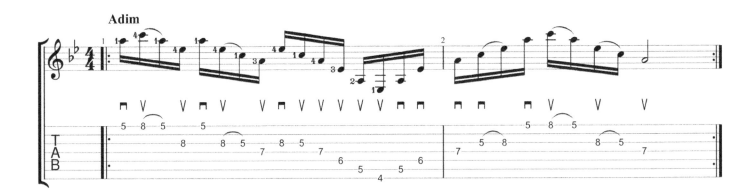

To create a little double turnaround madness and take advantage of the 4-3-2-1 fingerings within some of the shapes, Example 8r bounces between the 4th and 11th positions with a flurry of diminished 5ths and root notes. This lick is not exactly high art, so have fun with the absurdity of it at high speed and be sure to listen to the audio!

Example 8r:

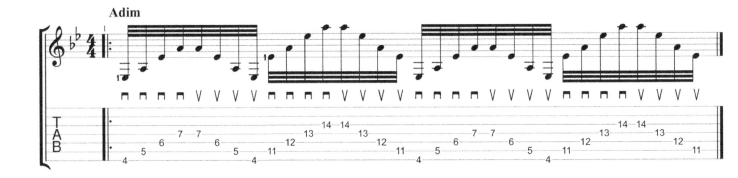

Speed Shapes for Suspended Chords – 1, 2, 5 and 1, 4, 5

Being neither major nor minor would exclude the basic suspended 2nd and 4th (*sus2* and *sus4*) chords from inclusion as triads in most theory books. They are included here due to their three-note construction. Suspended chords can resolve to either major or minor chords so long as the major 2nd or perfect 4th degree that replaces the 3rd of the chord fits within the key signature at hand.

Suspended 4th chords occur diatonically at degrees I, II, III, V and VI of the major scale. Suspended 2nd chords can be generated from the I, II, IV, V and VI degrees.

Suspended 2nd and 4th chords can be viewed as inversions of each other from different root notes. For Example, Asus4 (A, D, E) shares the same notes as Dsus2 (D, E, A). Only one set of speed shapes is required as a result, applied according to the chord at hand. In another example of this connecting point of view, an Asus2 chord (A, B, E) contains the same notes as an Esus4 chord (E, A, B).

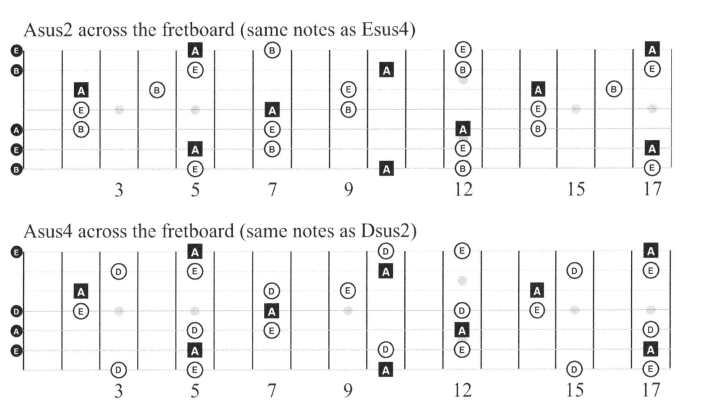

The 1-1-2-1-1-1-2 string layout works for Speed Shape 1 of the suspended triad. Speed Shape 2 for Asus4 would end up with an E note all the way over on the 7th fret of the A string, so I've relocated that note to the 12th fret of the low E string. Speed Shape 3 doesn't provide a particularly practical shape for most fretboard positions, so I like to combine elements of the second and third shapes into a hybrid pattern which includes a position shift when moving to the A string.

Sus4 Speed Shape 1

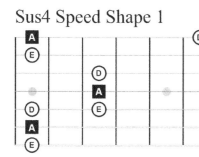

Sus4 Speed Shape 2

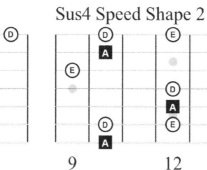

Sus4 Speed Shape 3

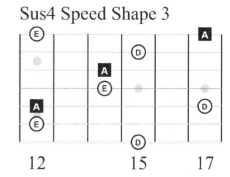

Shape 2/3 Hybrid

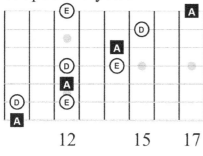

For the hybrid shape, repeat the fingering from the low B and low E strings on the A and D strings, initiating the 3rd string A note with the index finger.

Example 8s:

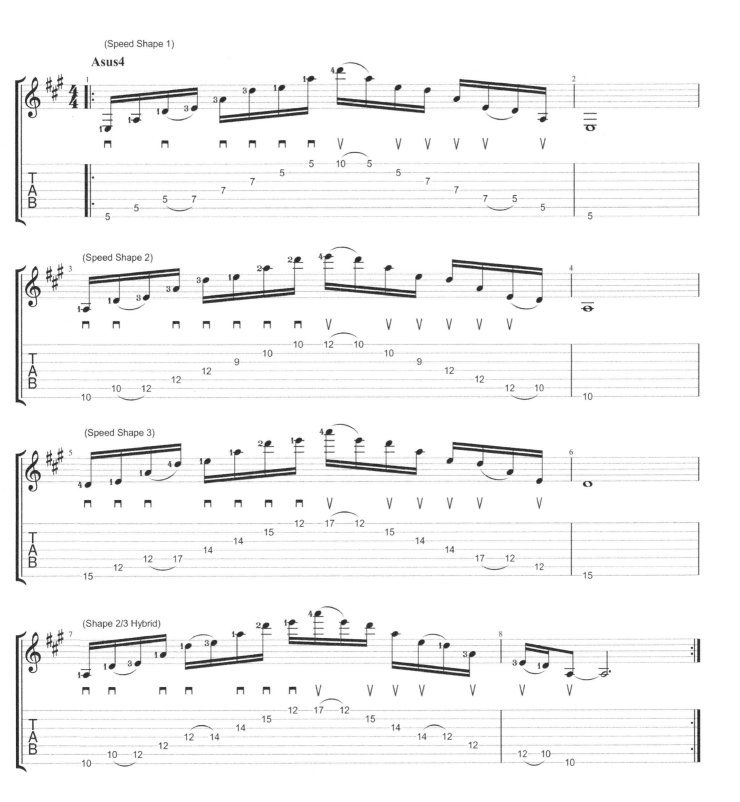

Playing Asus2 using the same shapes is merely a matter of taking the sus4 shapes and transposing them down a perfect 4th or up a perfect 5th. In Example 8t, the hybrid suspended shape is played from the 5th fret of the low B string to spell out an Asus2 triad.

Example 8t:

Speed Shape Monster Lick

The last example for this section combines major, augmented, minor and suspended chords in one lick that will test your fluency and ability to switch triads and inversions on the fly.

Example 8u:

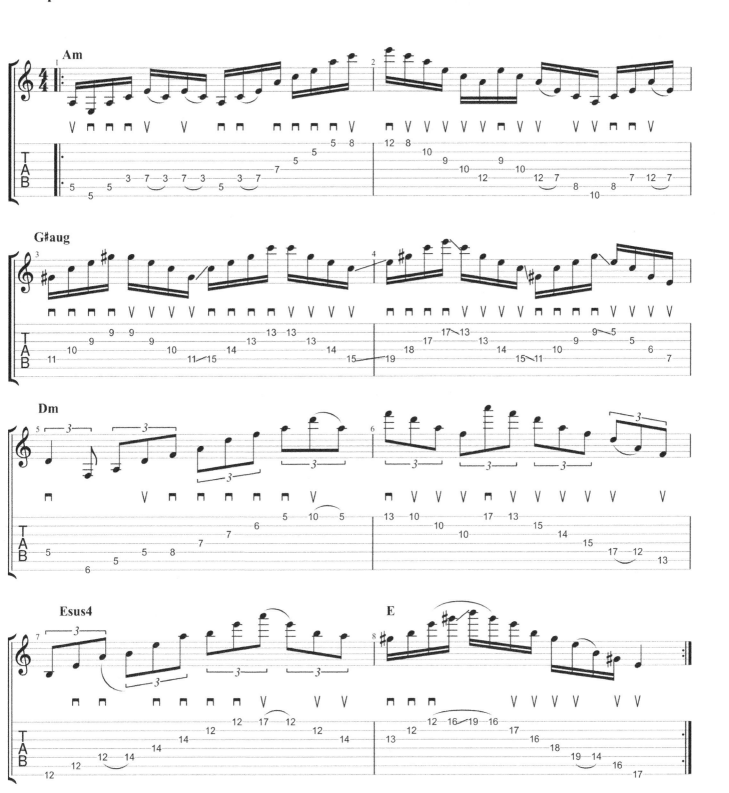

When you can play the above example, there's no excuse not to create your own material based on any chord progression you know or borrow from existing compositions. You have the chops. You have the layouts. It's time to make music!

Goal-setting for fretboard coverage

When arriving at the end of an ambitious chapter such as this, it can feel like an arduous task to refine all the information into a routine for development.

Obviously, practise the examples in the chapter, choosing a few at a time without mentally overloading yourself within a single practice session. Since you already have the necessary sweep picking mechanics at your disposal, the area of focus for this chapter should be on memorisation and application of the various chord types and inversions.

Next, ensure that you can complete the list of tasks below. For any areas in which you continue to struggle, refer to the relevant text and examples and then take a second or third attempt at the list.

Speed Shapes

- Memorise the three speed shapes of the major and minor triads, i.e. six patterns in total.

- Memorise augmented triads by switching between major and augmented shapes.

- Repeat the previous step for minor and diminished triads.

- Play each diatonic triad from the key of A Major using Speed Shape 1: A Major, B Minor, C# Minor, D Major, E Major, F# Minor, G# Diminished.

- Alternate between suspended 2nd and suspended 4th chords in each shape.

- Play each chord type from the same root note, then try the same with each inversion.

Composition

- Create your own etude using the chords A Major, B Minor, Esus4, E Major.

- Create your own etude using the chords F# Minor, F Augmented, A Major, B Major.

- Create your own etude using the chords B Minor, G# Diminished, G Major, D Major.

Chapter Nine: Fretboard Coverage – Sevenths

Arpeggiating beyond triads is a valuable device for adding colour to composition and improvisation, outlining upper extensions of basic chords and increasing your palette of sweep picking sounds. This chapter focuses on the addition of the VII degree above the triads discussed in Chapter Eight using seven-string speed shapes. With the addition of a chord tone comes an extra speed shape for seventh chords.

Chords covered in this section include major seventh, dominant seventh, minor seventh, half-diminished, and diminished seventh. Delving into these chords in the prescribed order provides a smooth transition with only one chord tone changing at a time.

Major Seventh Arpeggios – 1, 3, 5, 7

Major seventh chords occur at the I and IV degrees of major scale harmony and contain four notes, the last of which is a major 7th above the root note, or a major 3rd above the 5th.

Amaj7 across the fretboard

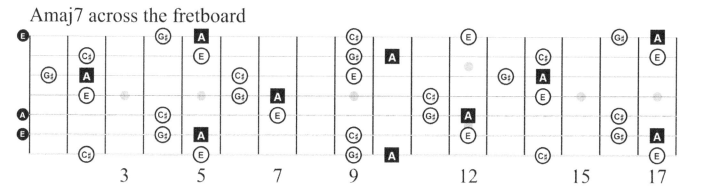

In the CAGED patterns, the most significant hurdles to achieving speed are the locations and proximity of certain occurrences of the notes E, G#, A and C# (in the key of A). These clusters require fingerings that are not always condusive to flow and agility, especially when relying on swift third and fourth finger switching.

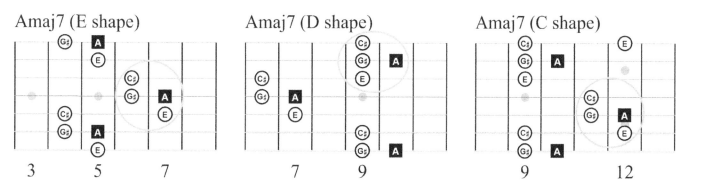

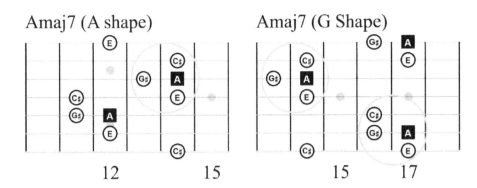

Amaj7 (A shape)   Amaj7 (G Shape)

Since seventh chords contain four notes, there will be four speed shapes for each arpeggio type. Each shape covers three octaves of the arpeggio in different inversions. Shapes 3 and 4 have the biggest spread across the fretboard but contain repeated shapes between the lowest and middle octaves. Each shape contains at least one slide from the 7th degree up to the next root note.

All of these factors help create smooth and fluid-sounding arpeggios at high speeds, so take your time learning your way around the shapes, even if they look a little confusing at first glance.

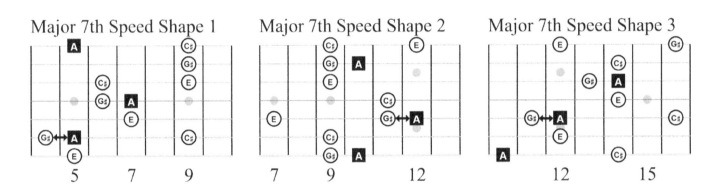

Major 7th Speed Shape 1   Major 7th Speed Shape 2   Major 7th Speed Shape 3

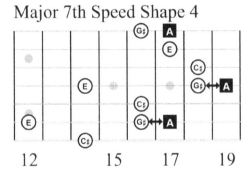

Major 7th Speed Shape 4

Seventh chord Speed Shapes feature some nice turnaround points, which Examples 9a through 9d take advantage of, complete with the fingerings I use for each. If you'd like a more aggressive sound, feel free to add more pickstrokes where slurs are indicated.

Example 9a: Major 7th Speed Shape 1

Example 9b: Major 7th Speed Shape 2

Example 9c: Major 7th Speed Shape 3

Example 9d: Major 7th Speed Shape 4

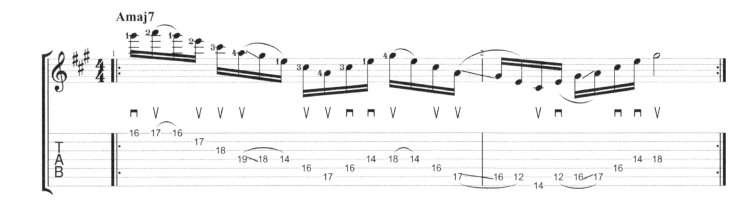

Dominant Seventh Arpeggios – 1, 3, 5, b7

Occurring on degree V of major, harmonic minor, and melodic minor scale harmony, the dominant seventh chord has a major quality with a minor or flatted 7th. In functional harmony, the 7th of the dominant chord will often resolve down one semitone to the 3rd of the tonic chord. Dominant chords are also extremely popular in modal vamps.

Mapping the dominant seventh chord can be done by lowering the 7th in the major seventh examples by one semitone. A dominant seventh chord with a root note of A has the chord symbol A7.

A7 across the fretboard

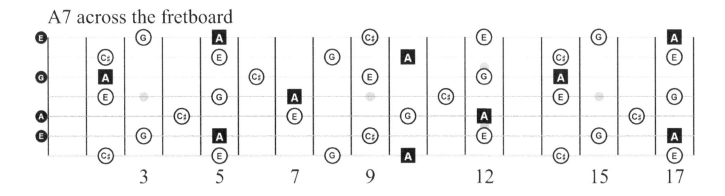

The four speed shapes for dominant seventh arpeggios use two-fret position slides since the 7th degree and the next root note are a whole tone apart. While the notes could be sourced from other strings, the slide approach – even with the bigger interval – is still an effective way to execute flurries of notes economically.

Dom. 7th Speed Shape 1

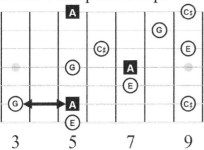

Dom. 7th Speed Shape 2

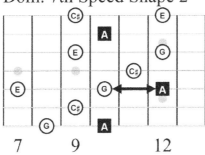

Dom. 7th Speed Shape 3

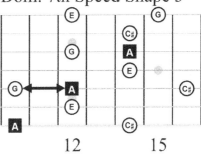

Dom. 7th Speed Shape 4

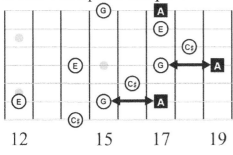

Speed Shapes 1, 3 and 4 have the same notes per string layout as their major seventh counterparts, but Speed Shape 2 sees the highest occurrence of the 7th degree placed on the G string instead of the high B string for convenience.

Following on from the first four examples of this chapter, Examples 9e to 9h use one pattern per lick, ascending and descending at various points to create musical interest.

Example 9e: Dominant 7th Speed Shape 1

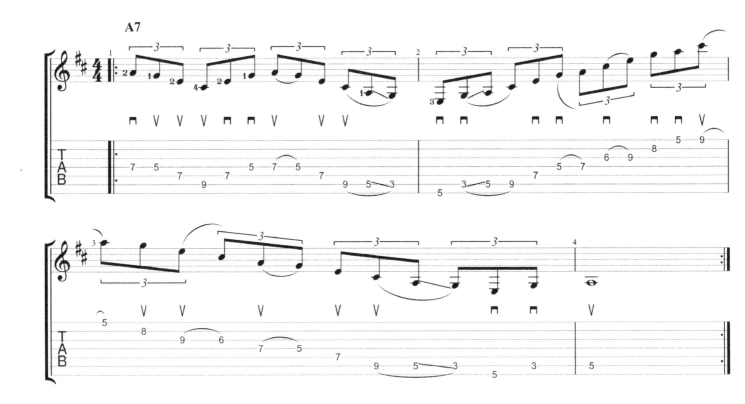

Example 9f: Dominant 7th Speed Shape 2

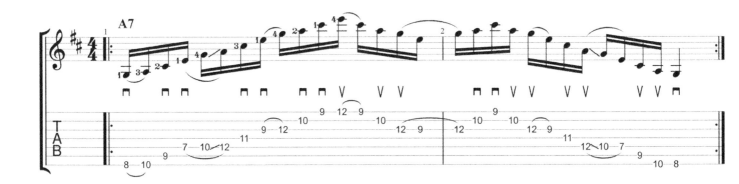

Example 9g: Dominant 7th Speed Shape 3

Example 9h: Dominant 7th Speed Shape 4

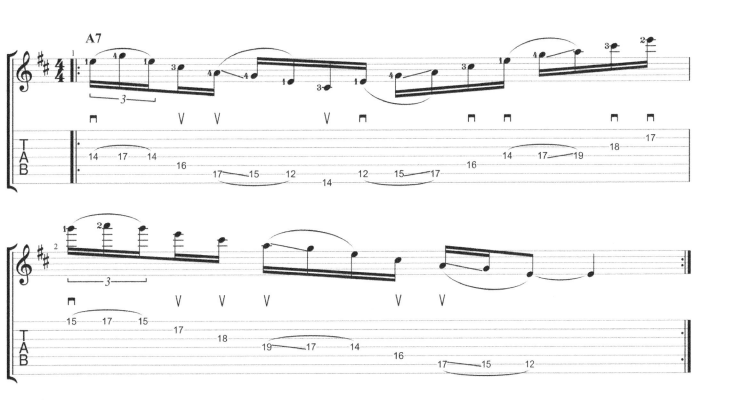

Minor Seventh Arpeggios – 1, b3, 5, b7

Found at the II, III, and VI degrees of major scale harmony, minor seventh chords consist of minor 3rd intervals between the root and 3rd and between the 5th and 7th, in addition to perfect 5th intervals between the root and 5th and between the 3rd and 7th. The first inversion of the minor seventh chord consists of the same notes as a major 6th chord. For example, an Am7 chord (A, C, E, G) contains the same notes as a C6 chord (C, E, G, A).

Am7 across the fretboard

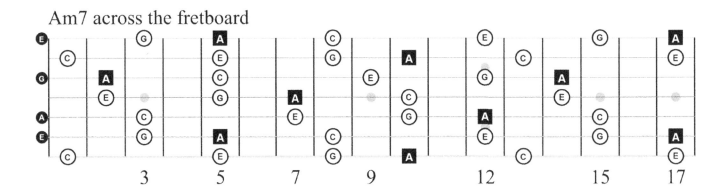

With the work you have already completed on the speed shapes of the major seventh and dominant seventh arpeggios, you should now be quite familiar with the picking hand mechanics of the four patterns, allowing focus on the fretting hand modifications for each new chord that comes along.

The speed shapes of minor 7th chords flatten the 3rd of each dominant seventh shape used previously.

Am7 Speed Shape 1   Am7 Speed Shape 2   Am7 Speed Shape 3

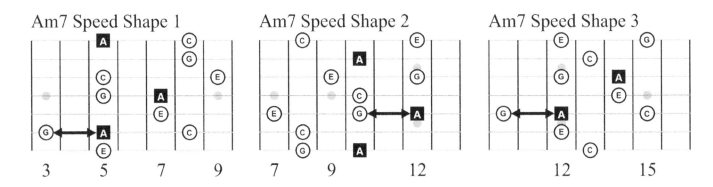

Am7 Speed Shape 4

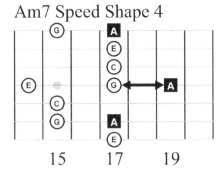

90

Speed Shape 1 for minor seventh arpeggios may remind you of a minor pentatonic scale, since it contains four of the five pentatonic notes. In bar one, beat 2, the G note on the 5th fret of the low E string could also be played on the 8th fret of the low B string to avoid position slides.

Example 9i:

Example 9j is a reminder of what a great pattern Speed Shape 2 is for almost all the arpeggio types. With a comfortable fingering in the lower octaves that really lends itself to some speed, this shape is hard to beat!

Example 9j:

Speed Shape 3 also reveals itself to be a user-friendly shape. In Example 9k, the twelve-note unit in bar one, beats 1 to 3 repeats an octave higher starting on beat 4. Both fragments work well in triplet note groupings too.

Example 9k:

To complete the minor seventh layouts, Speed Shape 4 in Example 9l begins with a descending slide on the way down to the lowest C note of the lick in the 13th fret of the low B string. Because the chords Am7 and Cmaj6 contain the same notes, this lick is a great one to bring out the major sixth flavour over a major chord.

Example 9l:

Half-diminished Arpeggios – 1, b3, b5, b7

The minor seventh (flat five) or *half-diminished* chord occurs in the harmonised major scale (VII), harmonic minor scale (VII) and melodic minor (VI and VII) scales. This chord differs from a minor seventh chord by way of its diminished 5th and is distinct from a *diminished seventh* chord by its b7 (instead of the bb7 of the diminished seventh).

Am7b5 across the fretboard

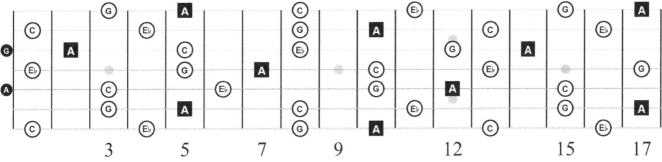

The transition from minor seventh to half-diminished triads using speed shapes is a smooth one. All shapes benefit from the visual cues provided by the low and middle octaves of each pattern. The notes of an Am7b5 chord (A, C, Eb, G) are the same as Cm6 (C, Eb, G, A), so these shapes can be used over the latter to invoke a Dorian mode tonality.

Minor 7b5 Speed Shape 1

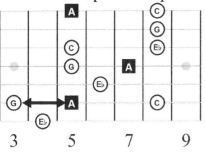

Minor 7b5 Speed Shape 2

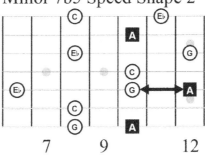

Minor 7b5 Speed Shape 3

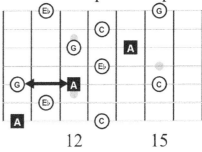

Minor 7b5 Speed Shape 4

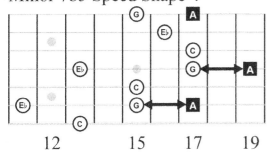

Examples 9m to 9p follow the same sequence as their speed shape counterparts in Examples 9i to 9l but are adjusted to represent the sounds of half-diminished arpeggios.

Example 9m:

Example 9n:

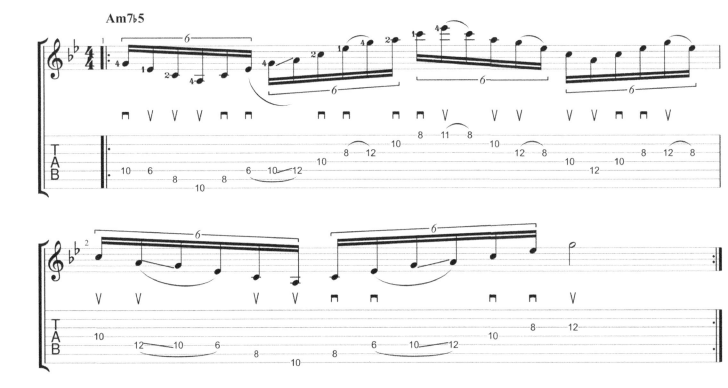

Example 9o:

Example 9p:

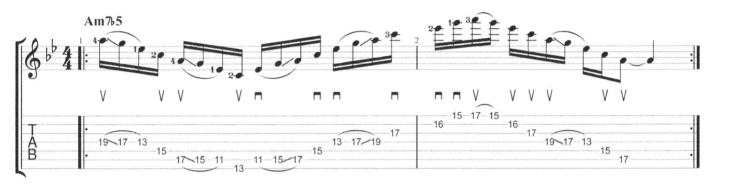

If the whole-tone spread between the D string and G string in Speed Shape 4 is uncomfortable, reposition the highest G note on the E string, 15th fret to the B string, 20th fret, adjusting the fingering to the following:

Minor 7b5 Speed Shape 4

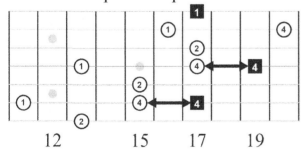

Once you've decided on a favourite option, retool Example 9p to suit, if necessary.

Diminished Seventh Arpeggios - 1, b3, b5, bb7

As covered in my book *Neoclassical Speed Strategies for Guitar*, diminished seventh arpeggios are formed by stacking consecutive minor 3rd intervals. There are also two diminished 5th intervals between the root and 5th, and between the 3rd and 7th of the chord.

Because of the repeated minor 3rd intervals, each inversion of the diminished seventh chord is a new chord unto itself. Geometrically, this keeps things very simple since we can choose our favourite shapes and move them up and down in multiples of three frets to cover the fretboard. Even when looking at the entire fretboard of diminished seventh intervals, it's easy to visualise the repeats of any given pattern.

Adim7 across the fretboard

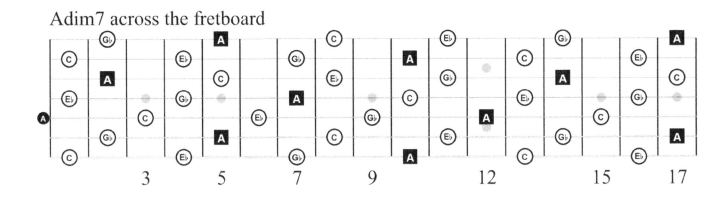

Due to the inversion attributes of diminished 7th chords, the Adim7 examples in this chapter can be used in conjunction with the scales of Bb Harmonic Minor, Db Harmonic Minor, E Harmonic Minor and G Harmonic Minor as a substitute for the V chord in any of those keys.

Other options avail themselves with some exploration of the fretboard, and since the chord tones are so evenly spread across the neck, moving between notes can be like a *Choose Your Own Adventure* book.

Here are just a few ways of cutting through three octaves of Adim7 using different patterns.

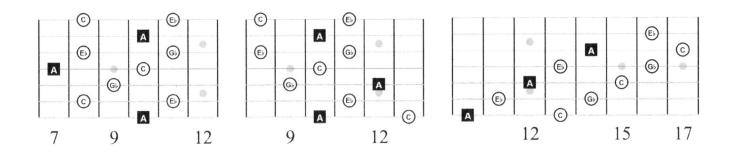

Example 9q:

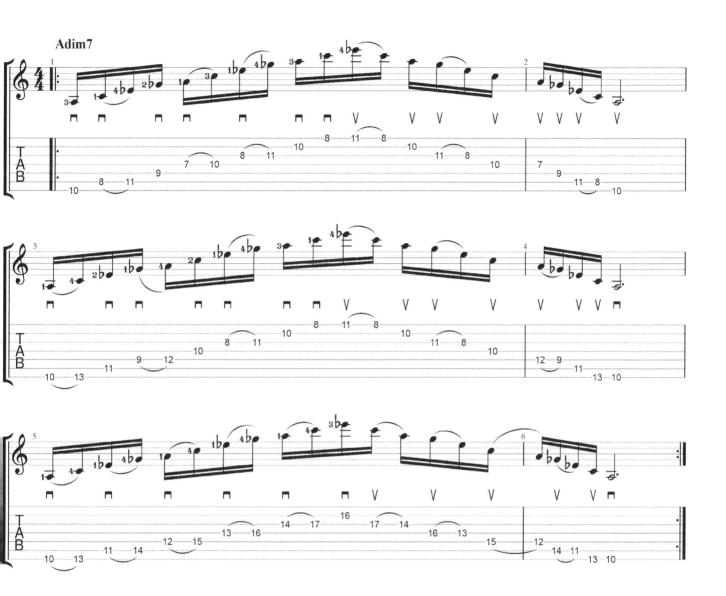

Once you've decided upon your favourite pattern, moving through inversions is done by shifting up and down in minor 3rd leaps. Example 9r demonstrates these jumps using various numbers of strings within the same movable shape.

Example 9r:

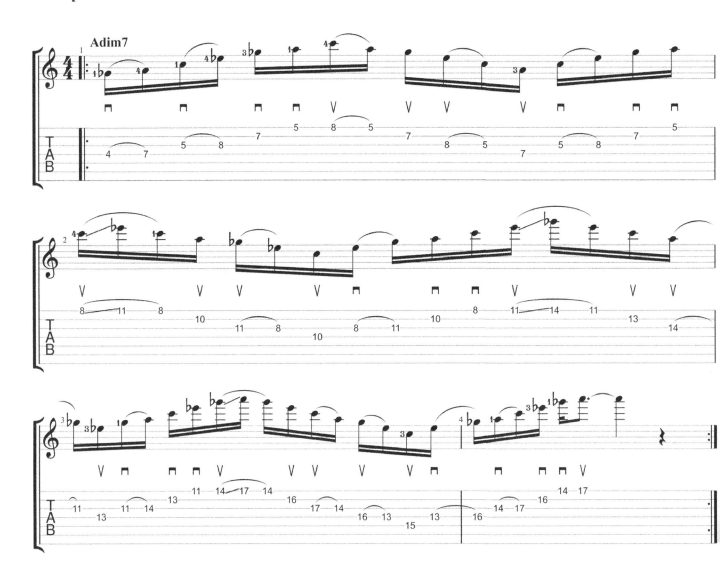

Three-octave Super Shapes

I call this last group of patterns *Super Shapes* because they move through octaves in a way that is easy to visualise and play at moderate to high speeds using sweep picking and slides. The aim is to examine the first four notes of any arpeggio, locate the same or similar shape one octave and two octaves higher, then join them with position shift slides.

The first octave of Speed Shape 2 accomplishes this nicely for the five chord types analysed in this chapter, especially for the minor family arpeggios. Take a look at the diagram for the Minor 7th Super Shape as you run through this process:

Play the first octave the same as our previous Speed Shape 2 examples, including the slide that takes you to the middle octave. Rather than fretting the two notes on the G string in-position, slide from the first note to the second note with the index finger. This shift will bring you into position for the highest octave. The geometry of each octave is almost the same, changing only on the high B and high E strings because of the major 3rd interval between the second and third string tuning. Repeat this for the other chord types as illustrated in the diagrams.

Examples 9s to 9w demonstrate the fingering and picking for each of the Shape 2-based super shapes.

Minor 7th Super Shape

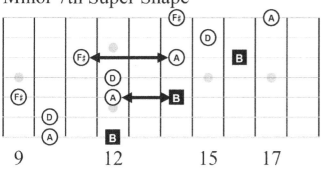

Minor 7b5 Super Shape

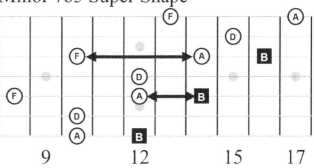

Diminished 7th Super Shape

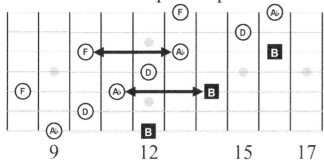

Major 7th Super Shape

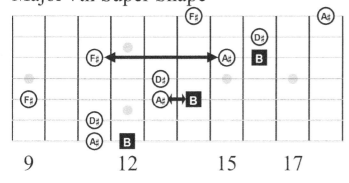

Dominant 7th Super Shape

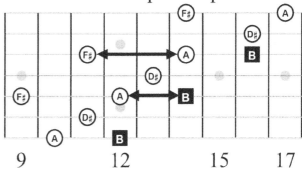

Example 9s:

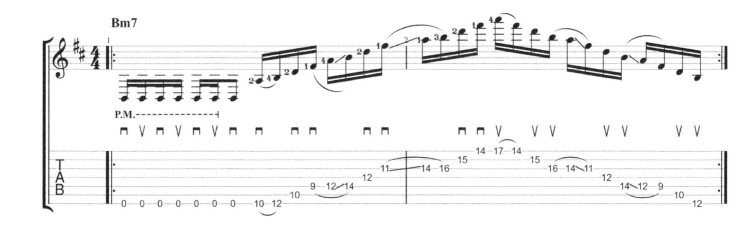

Example 9t:

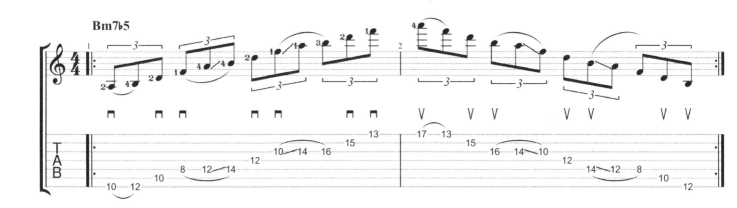

Example 9u:

Example 9v:

Example 9w:

When you can play these examples, examine the fretboard maps for each chord type and see if you can locate other octave-shifting patterns for your favourite arpeggio types.

How to Practise Chapter Nine

The aim of this chapter has been to arm you with speed shapes that have more commonalities than differences. The order of the arpeggios presented has been quite deliberate in the way that each chord type differs from the one before it, and the one after it, by one note each time.

To make the most of the step-by-step approach of modulating from major seventh arpeggios through to diminished arpeggios, I suggest that your practice consists of three stages for this material.

1. Practise each arpeggio using its four speed shapes.

2. Practice each speed shape using every chord type before moving to the next shape.

3. Experiment with the Super Shapes in various arpeggio types.

Once you have committed these shapes to memory and have developed the facility to change chord types and inversions at will, look at the etudes in Chapter Ten.

Chapter Ten: Seventh Arpeggio Etudes

This chapter presents six etudes that explore seventh arpeggios, each with a slightly different objective and style of delivery. On the accompanying audio, each etude is played at full speed with the backing track, then at a slower speed unaccompanied.

The first etude has a prog rock feel and is designed to help you compare different arpeggios from the same root note with the modulation from Gmaj7 to Gm7 and again from Fmaj7 to Fm7.

Example 10a:

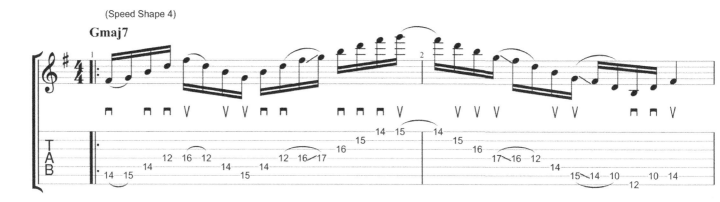

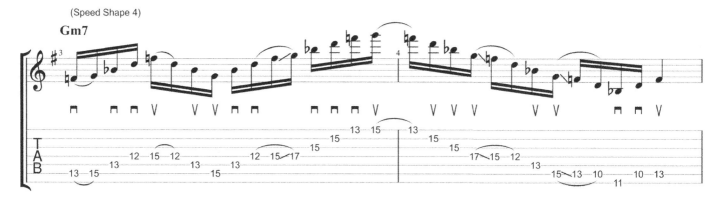

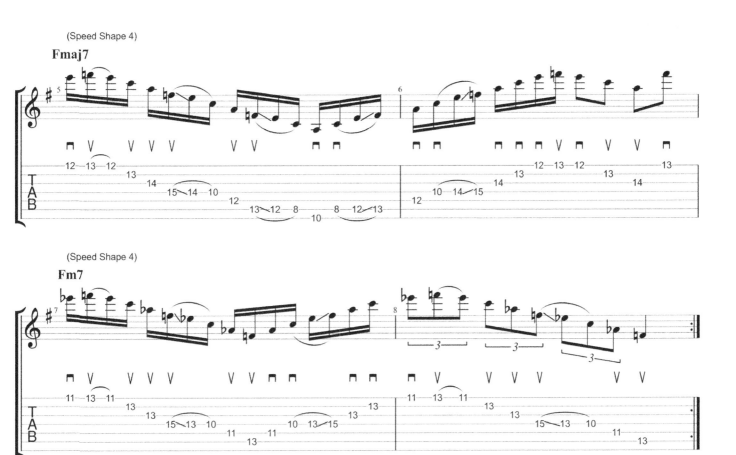

Example 10b is written in the style of neoclassical rock players like Vinnie Moore. Using a moving chord progression diatonic to B Minor, this etude uses the same chord sequence twice, but with different inversions the second time. In the notation of the C#dim7 arpeggios, you'll see A# notes in the place of Bb (bb7) in accordance with the B Harmonic Minor scale.

Example 10b:

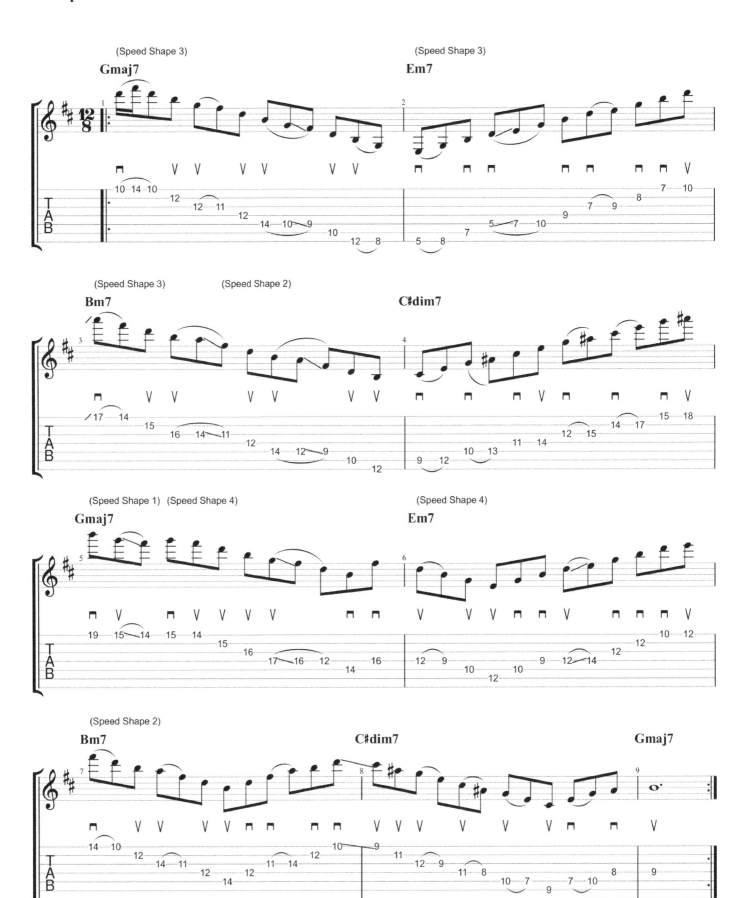

Written with a country feel in mind and comprised solely of dominant seventh chords, the third etude in this chapter will have you switching arpeggios within a smaller range of fretboard space. Comprised of the speed shapes notes above each chord, we have a I, IV, V progression for the first six bars. The seventh and eighth bars feature a turnaround.

In anticipation of the first chord change from A7 to D7, the last note of bar two is a C natural note. Not only does this make fretting easier for the index finger through the change, it also allows smooth modulation between the tonalities of the two chords.

Example 10c:

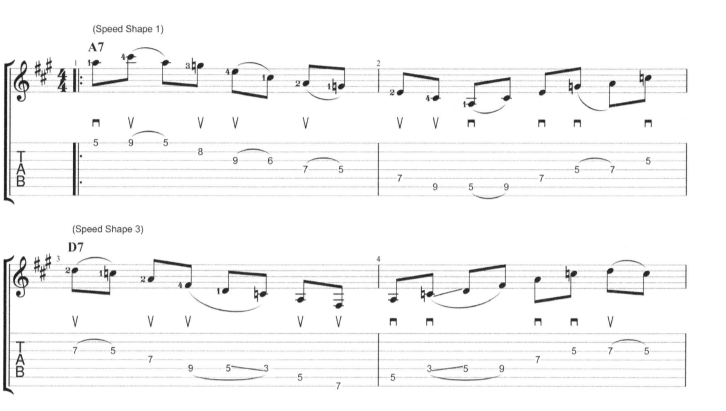

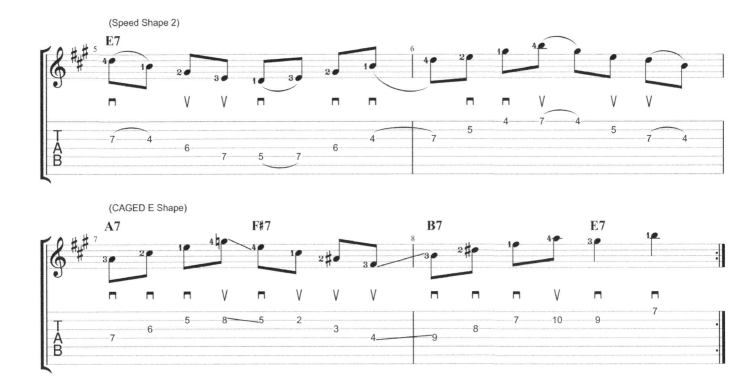

Example 10d uses the second speed shapes of Am7 and C7, the fourth speed shape of Fmaj7 and the third speed shape of Fm7. Despite the changing fingering forms, the etude uses the same melodic sequence for descending and ascending within each arpeggio, breaking early in the fourth bar before the repeat. Some common tones connect the arpeggios, with all four chords containing a C note, and three of the chords containing an E (which becomes Eb in bar four).

Example 10d:

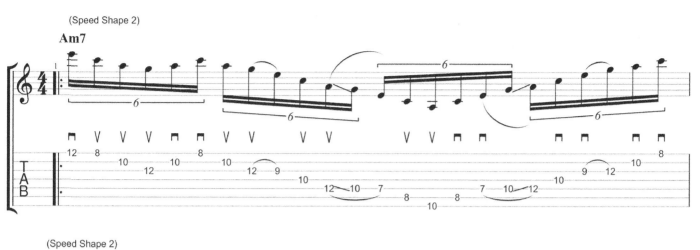

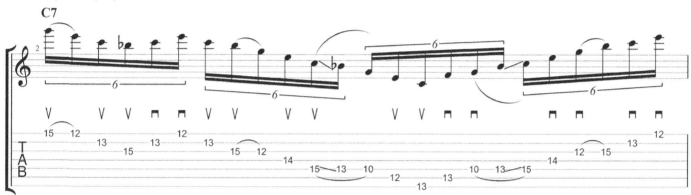

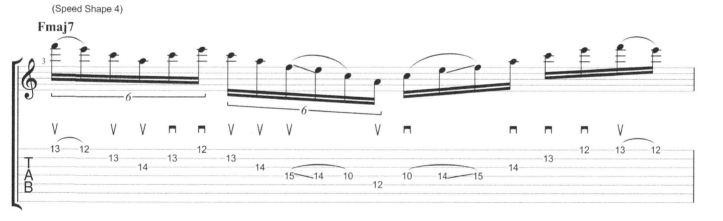

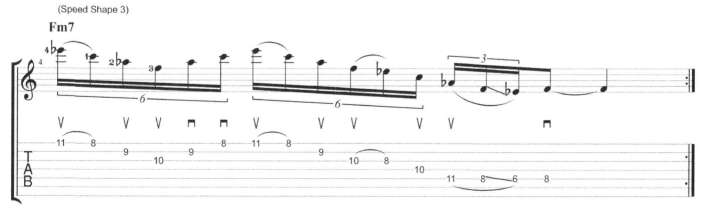

Introducing some syncopation to sweep picking lines allows us to break free of the notion that sweeping needs to be about a barrage of notes. Rests allow a sense of clever phrasing within your lines. The next etude in B Minor has a funk-fusion vibe with even a little Latin influence, and rests in each bar.

Where rests occur, aim for silence in those spaces rather than letting the previous notes hang over. To punctuate the rests, try adding a little extra oomph to the preceding picked note in each instance.

Example 10e:

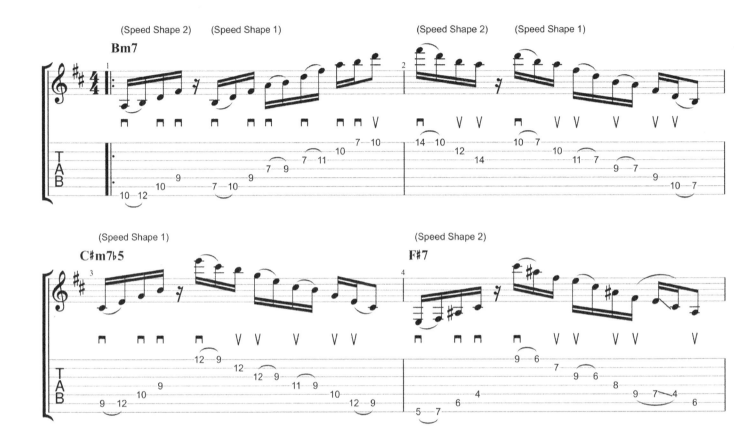

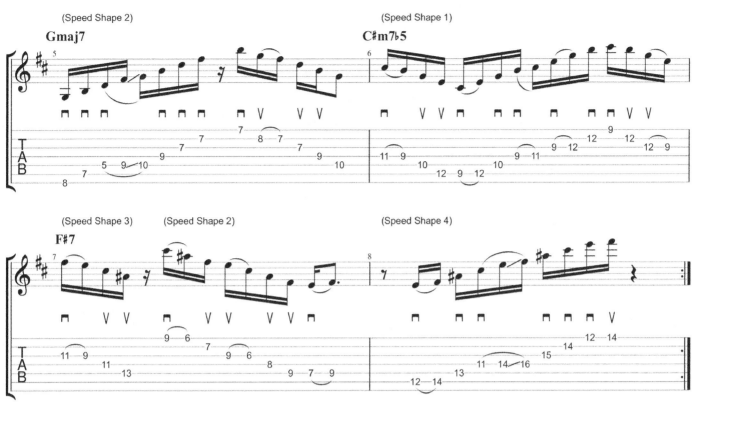

The final etude has a prog-rock feel in 5/4 time. Using the III and IV chords from the key of F Major, this example uses three speed shapes per arpeggio. In bar one, Speed Shapes 2 and 3 of Am7 connect at the beginning of beat 3 using an upward index finger slide. In bar two, the shape change occurs on the last 1/16th note of beat 3 with a downward index finger slide. The changes for Bbmaj7 occur at the same points within the two-bar sequence (bars three and four).

Example 10f:

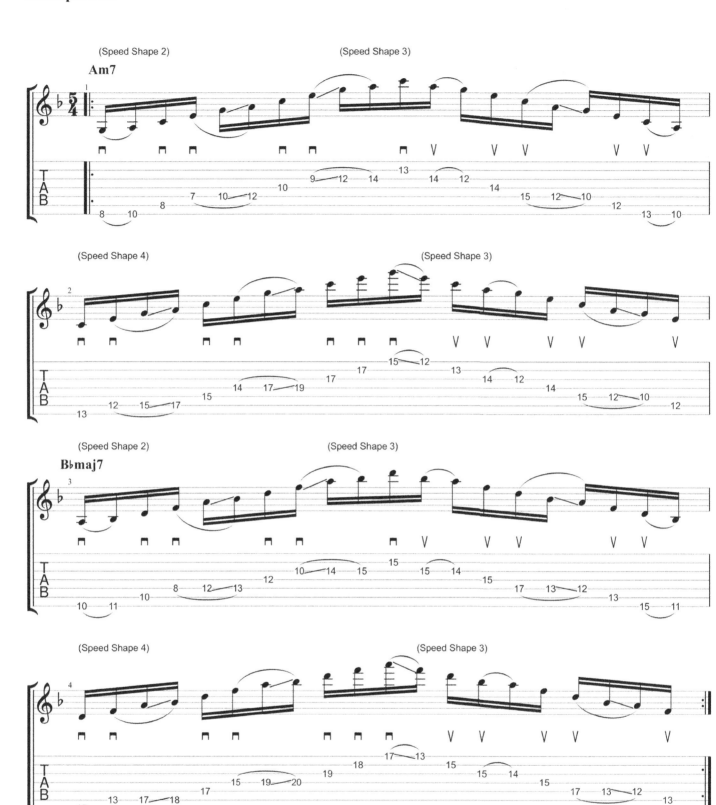

Long term practice goals

Instead of rehashing the essentials of practice that have been cited in previous chapters, this *How to Practise* section contains a checklist of *essential attributes* for your performance of the examples provided in this book. You're making real music with sweep picking now, so it's important to aim high with your delivery, be highly self-aware, and honest with yourself about any areas of weakness.

When performing the etudes of this chapter, and indeed all drills and etudes in the book, can you:

- Ascend and descend with equal facility?

- Play in time when combining picked notes and slurs?

- Control the strings in use while silencing the others?

- Change positions without affecting the tempo?

- Apply dynamic effects like picking accents and muted notes at will?

- Play through examples at a constant tempo with a metronome or drum beat?

- Find and track your top clean tempo for future comparison?

If all the above received a tick, you are becoming the sweep picker I know you can be! If not, keep working. You will get there. By focusing your practice on the end game, you have a gauge by which to judge your progress. Check the above list from time to time to remind yourself what you're working towards.

Chapter Eleven – Approaching Drop A Tuning for Triads and Arpeggios

Drop A tuning for seven-string guitar (A-E-A-D-G-B-E) opens up some cool options for rhythm playing, like one-finger power chords on the lower strings, wide interval chord voicings, and the visual convenience of having the same notes (an octave apart) on the seventh and fifth strings.

Melodic concepts like arpeggios in drop tunings can throw some players off, leading them to avoid the seventh string altogether in improvisation. Lowering the seventh string down by a whole tone certainly makes some notes a little tricker to reach but makes others easier.

The shapes in this chapter are designed to avoid disruption to the other six strings in the location of notes. There are just a couple of changes to fingerings. Changing too much can create a domino effect, sending you back to the drawing board on arpeggio shapes, and you won't want that if you're a player who switches between standard and drop tunings.

For major, minor, augmented and diminished triads along with suspended arpeggios, each seventh-string note has moved up two frets, and fingering modifications have been noted on the relevant strings. For minor triads in Speed Shape 2, I break the modification rule by moving the E note in an A Minor triad from the higher A string to the low E string.

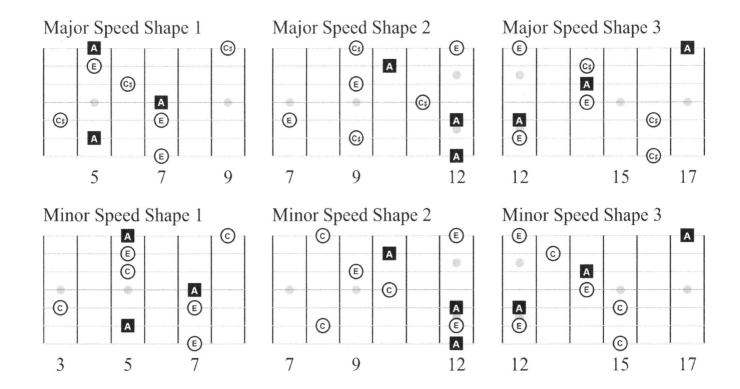

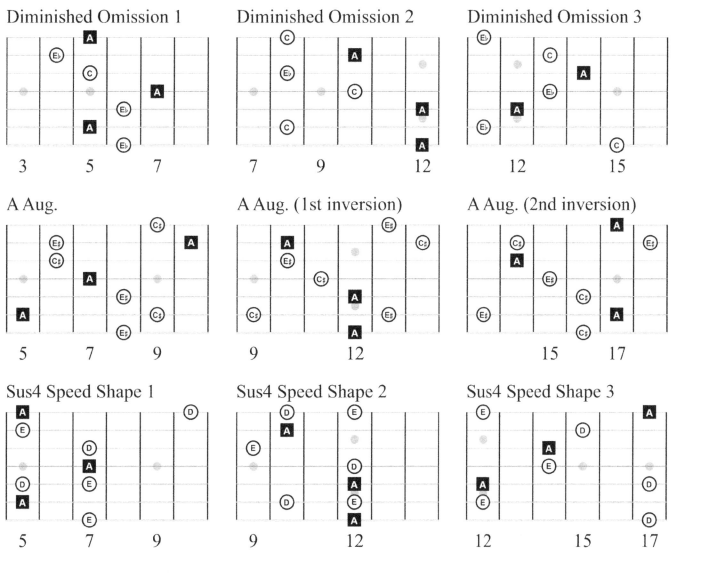

Diminished Omission 1

Diminished Omission 2

Diminished Omission 3

A Aug.

A Aug. (1st inversion)

A Aug. (2nd inversion)

Sus4 Speed Shape 1

Sus4 Speed Shape 2

Sus4 Speed Shape 3

Applying drop tuning to the four speed shapes for seventh arpeggios means some notes become easily accessible, but others become inconvenient. To help you visualise the changes and potential workarounds, take a look at each of the new major seventh arpeggio shapes as you read the points that follow.

- Speed Shape 1: the 3rd of the chord is now within reach and can be added to the beginning of the arpeggio.

- Speed Shape 2: the 5th of the chord is now accessible and has been added to the shape but reaching the root note is awkward. We can use the 5th and 7th degrees on the seventh string in an omission shape instead. Omitted notes are included but have been greyed.

- Speed Shape 3: the 3rd is now awkward to reach without making changes to other strings (which we're trying to avoid). I play these as omission shapes using the fingerings provided to keep the other strings as-is, but you could move the 7th of these shapes to the low E string if desired for less of a sweep-sounding shape and more of a legato idea.

- Speed Shape 4: the root note of the chord is now accessible and can be used to begin the arpeggio.

Major 7th Speed Shape 1

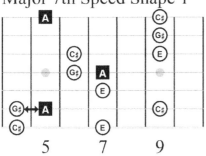

5   7   9

Major 7th Speed Shape 2

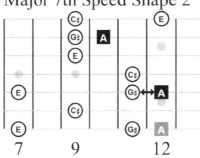

7   9   12

Major 7th Speed Shape 3

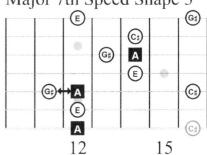

12   15

Major 7th Speed Shape 4

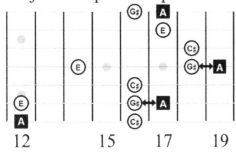

12   15   17   19

Dom. 7th Speed Shape 1

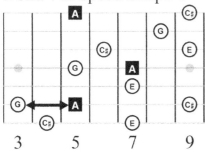

3   5   7   9

Dom. 7th Speed Shape 2

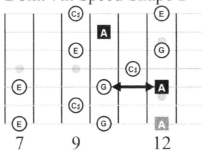

7   9   12

Dom. 7th Speed Shape 3

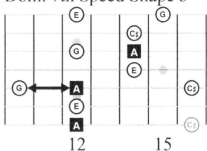

12   15

Dom. 7th Speed Shape 4

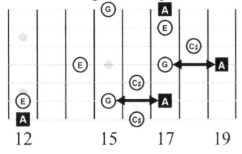

12   15   17   19

Minor 7th Speed Shape 1

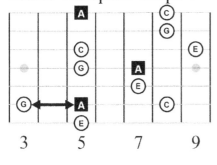

3   5   7   9

Minor 7th Speed Shape 2

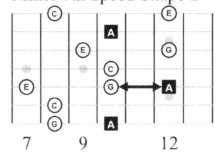

7   9   12

Minor 7th Speed Shape 3

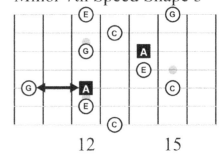

12   15

Minor 7th Speed Shape 4

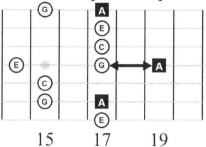

Minor 7b5 Speed Shape 1

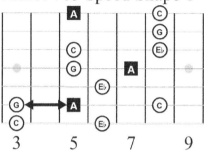

Minor 7b5 Speed Shape 2

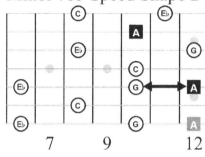

Minor 7b5 Speed Shape 3

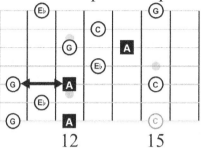

Minor 7b5 Speed Shape 4

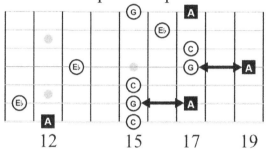

For diminished seventh arpeggios, the shifting of seventh-string notes is straightforward. Here are the modded versions of shapes we used in Chapter Eight.

Diminished 7th

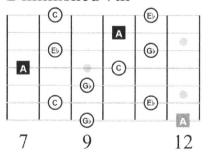

Diminished 7th

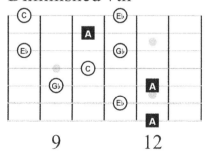

Diminished 7th

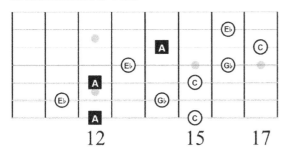

How to adapt licks in this book to drop tuning

You can get acquainted with the adjusted shapes by focusing on the lower strings briefly. Example 11a targets strings five, six and seven in the three shapes for an A Major triad.

Example 11a:

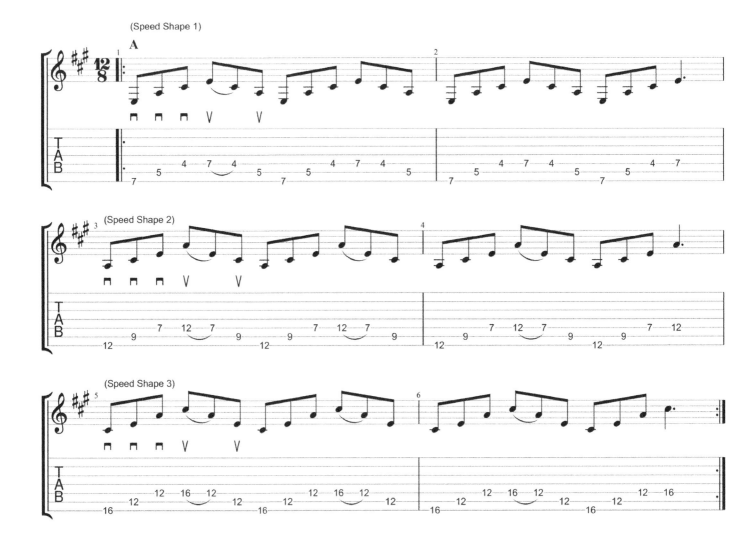

When you've memorised the new locations of the seventh-string notes, bring whole shapes back into play. Example 11b does this using the lower portion and then the complete shape of A Major, Speed Shape 1. When looping the bottom fragment versus playing the whole arpeggio, feel free to use alternate fingerings for the 7th fret of the higher A string e.g., the fourth finger when looping and the third finger when ascending or descending in full.

Example 11b:

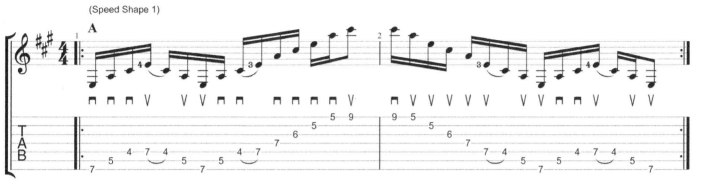

After some practice with the drop tuning shapes, start thinking more about the melodic shape of the lines you're playing rather than fret numbers. You don't necessarily have to read sheet music to do this, but you'll notice that the notation for standard tuning and Drop A tunings remain the same.

Here is the previous example, written in standard tuning. Same notes, different fret on the seventh string.

Example 11b2:

For examples written around standard tuning shapes that are no longer as convenient in drop tuning (seventh arpeggios in Shape 2, for example), look at where the licks rise or fall in pitch and try to apply a similar musical curve using the new shapes. You'll end up with a couple of different notes but the same musical intent.

In standard tuning, Example 9b used Speed Shape 2 of Amaj7 and went like this:

Example 9b (reprise) in standard tuning:

Using the drop tuning omission shape from this chapter, we can create a lick which serves a similar purpose musically without feeling like a game of *Twister*.

Example 11c:

If you still need a little practice adapting licks from previous chapters to Drop A tuning, you can pencil in changes underneath the tablature if you are working from a printed edition of this book, or transcribe your favourite licks into notation programs like Sibelius or Guitar Pro, adjusting the fret numbers along the seventh string. For any other tunings you may wish to use, try the same approach of finding the happy medium between musical intent and playability.

Conclusion

As you might have gathered through my books, I'm a big believer in strategy. It almost doesn't matter what your approach is, so long as you have one and it serves you. Strategy is what turns aimless into purposeful. It's the plan that kicks into action when you need it.

Besides the biomechanical, musical, geometric and theoretical information presented in this book, my biggest hope for this book is that it gives you the confidence to break down any aspect of guitar performance in a solutions-oriented manner.

What are my options?

Which one works best for me?

How can I take the optimal solution and use it to create a hundred new ideas?

These are the questions to ask yourself with any concept.

While it's important to me as an educator that the material in this book resonates with you and inspires your arpeggio execution systems, it's also okay to disagree with me! Do you like to pick notes that I hammered on? Do you wish to use outside picking where I opted for inside picking? Examine the reasoning and put it into practice. If it works best for you, then it's the right way for you.

However carefully you align with, or diverge from, the strategies in this book, the key is to know what you like, why you prefer it, and to be consistent in your application. That way, *your* system emerges, serving your aims and personalising a well-considered approach to your own playing.

It's been an absolute pleasure to present this material to you.

About the Author

Chris Brooks is a guitarist, educator and recording artist based in Sydney, Australia. What began as an obsession with '80s high octane lead guitar has, well, not changed at all.

A former student of the Australian Institute of Music, Brooks exhibited an early penchant for guitar-driven music, whether it was the sideman shredding of Kee Marcello and Brett Garsed, or the solo-artist career paths of Vinnie Moore, Steve Vai and Yngwie Malmsteen. The obligatory eight-hour practice sessions would be fuelled by lesson material from Hot Licks and REH videos as Brooks followed the trajectory to making his own guitar music.

Releasing two solo albums, 2002's *The Master Plan* and 2011's *The Axis of All Things*, Chris has received acclaim from print and online media worldwide, including Japan where *The Master Plan* was included in *Young Guitar* magazine's *500 Essential Guitar Albums* special issue, and back home in Australia where *Australian Guitar* magazine rated him one of the top underground guitarists.

Brooks has also recorded with *Yngwie Malmsteen*'s former vocalist *Mark Boals*, Australian melodic metal band *LORD*, toured with major label band *Feeding the Addiction*, and appeared on compilation albums for labels including Frontiers (Europe), Marquee Inc. (Japan) and Liquid Note Records (UK).

As founder of **guitarlickstore.com**, Brooks has created popular guitar courses including *Sweep Picking Systems for Arpeggios*, *Picking Systems for Pentatonic*, and *The Yng Way*. The latter proved to be the impetus for Brooks' first book for Fundamental Changes entitled *Neoclassical Speed Strategies for Guitar*.

With a keen eye for the detail of what makes things work on the guitar, and an aversion to sleep, Brooks is working towards a large body of educational resources and musical output.

Neoclassical Speed Strategies for Guitar is the result of 27 years studying Neoclassical guitar and one of the most influential pickers in guitar history. These principles will help you develop perfect guitar technique for any style. You'll master picking biomechanics, technique, theory and hundreds of licks to turn you into a shred guitar monster!

- Master the Neoclassical speed-picking system

- A definitive study of speed techniques and biomechanics for shred guitar

- A systematic guide to fast picking and string-change strategies

- Master the 9 principles of speed-picking as they're dissected, analysed and applied

- Complete technical development through over 90 real-life musical examples and "In the Style of" Licks

- 18 original Yngwie-inspired Neoclassical studies to build guitar technique and consolidate every essential speed-picking principle

Other Rock Guitar Books from Fundamental Changes

100 Classic Rock Licks for Guitar

Beyond Rhythm Guitar

Complete Technique for Modern Guitar

Exotic Pentatonic Soloing for Guitar

First Chord Progressions for Guitar

Funk Guitar Mastery

Guitar Chords in Context

Guitar Fretboard Fluency

Guitar Scales in Context

Heavy Metal Guitar Bible

Heavy Metal Lead Guitar

Heavy Metal Rhythm Guitar

Progressive Metal Guitar

Rock Guitar Un-CAGED

Rock Rhythm Guitar Playing

The Circle of Fifths for Guitarists

The Complete DADGAD Guitar Method

The Complete Guide to Playing Blues Guitar Book One: Rhythm Guitar

The Complete Guide to Playing Blues Guitar Book Three: Beyond Pentatonics

The Complete Guide to Playing Blues Guitar Book Two: Melodic Phrasing

The Complete Guide to Playing Blues Guitar Compilation

The Complete Technique, Theory & Scales Compilation for Guitar

The First 100 Chords for Guitar

The Practical Guide to Modern Music Theory for Guitarists

Neoclassical Speed Strategies for Guitar

Made in the USA
Monee, IL
02 September 2024

65058181R00070